T0304919

THE ATLAS OF

BOURBON

& AMERICAN WHISKEY

Dedication

For Giorgio and Elio

First published in Great Britain in 2021 by Mitchell Beazley,
an imprint of Octopus Publishing Group Ltd,
Carmelite House, 50 Victoria Embankment,
London EC4Y 0DZ
www.octopusbooks.co.uk
www.octopusbooksusa.com

An Hachette UK Company
www.hachette.co.uk

Design and layout copyright © Octopus Publishing Group 2021
Text copyright © Eric Zandona 2021

Distributed in the US by Hachette Book Group,
1290 Avenue of the Americas, 4th and 5th Floors,
New York, NY 10104

Distributed in Canada by Canadian Manda Group,
664 Annette St., Toronto, Ontario, Canada M6S 2C8

ISBN 978-1-78472-740-6

A CIP catalogue record for this book is available from the British Library.

Printed and bound in China.

10 9 8 7 6 5 4 3 2 1

Editorial Director: Joe Cottington
Art Director: Juliette Norsworthy
Senior Editor: Leanne Bryan
Copyeditor: Jo Richardson
Designer: Geoff Fennell
Picture Researchers: Giulia Hetherington and Jennifer Veall
Illustrator: Dave Hopkins
Production Controller: Serena Savini

THE ATLAS OF

BOURBON

&

AMERICAN WHISKEY

A JOURNEY THROUGH
THE SPIRIT OF AMERICA

ERIC ZANDONA

MITCHELL BEAZLEY

Contents

Introduction

In its own way, whiskey tells the history of the United States – its regional quirks and differences are born out of historical events, local climate and the particular tastes of a given area. Taken together, they form a distinct and unique part of the country's culture. Taken individually, there is a wealth of different whiskeys to enjoy.

US law allows any style of whiskey to be made in any state, yet regional styles developed shortly after the founding of the country, only to disappear in the 19th century and then re-emerge in the 21st. While early regional styles of whiskey developed based on which crops grew well in a given area, contemporary efforts to codify and recreate these styles draw not only on the practicality of crop cultivation but also to celebrate the range of flavours that comes from making whiskey in different regions and maturing it in different climates.

This atlas provides a quick primer on the history of bourbon and American whiskey, and a brief technical

overview of what makes American whiskey unique, before diving into a more in-depth look at each region. Since the number of regional styles continues to grow, this book is not intended as an exhaustive mapping of American whiskey, rather an overview of the key regional styles including four regional variations of bourbon, four variations of rye whiskey, smoked whiskeys distilled in the Southern states and American single malt whiskeys from the Pacific Northwest. Each of these chapters will briefly cover the historical circumstances that led to the development of these key styles, how they are made, who makes them and tasting notes for examples of the style. The selection of distillers and whiskeys here is by no means complete – there is far more distilling talent and good whiskey than could be accommodated in the pages of this book – but will hopefully give you a snapshot of a given region, and a starting point for your exploration of it. And to help that exploration, each chapter ends with a suggested cocktail, one that has some historical or flavour connection to the region.

We are at an exciting moment in the history of American whiskey. There has never been a time when both the variety and quality of whiskeys have been greater. Distillers around the country are creating whiskeys informed by the grains, water and climate of their area, including many produced in regions beyond those featured in this book. But within these pages you will find the backbone of American whiskey – the historical centres, the modern-day hubs and the emerging styles that are driving the drink in the most interesting directions. So use this atlas to better understand, explore and taste the diversity of flavours to be found in bourbon and American whiskey.

A short history of regional American whiskeys

Over the past four centuries, distilling traditions in France and the British Isles slowly developed and solidified into what we recognize today as Armagnac, Cognac, Calvados, Scotch whisky and Irish whiskey. Today, these spirits have precise production requirements, and geographical boundaries codified by law and protected by international trade agreements. However, much of the history of these spirits took place in a pre-industrial era, which helped them develop their own unique traditions and methods bound in specific regions.

In contrast, American whiskey was born just a few short decades before industrialization transformed the country from an agrarian society to one of mostly wage labourers. As business and transportation networks were industrialized, it became cheaper to buy beef from Texas, cheese from Wisconsin and whiskey from Kentucky than from a local farmer, dairy or distiller, and a national market began to grow. Unsurprisingly, federal

Opposite: Backbar with Kentucky and Texas bourbon.

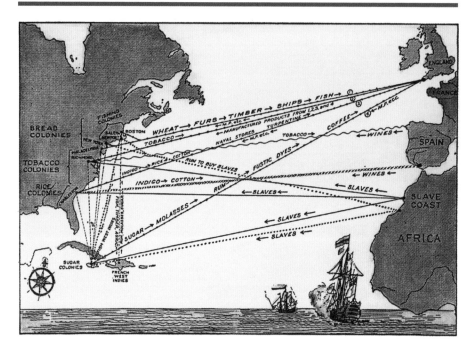

Above: Map of the 'triangular trade' between Britain, its American colonies and Africa in the 17th and 18th centuries.

law, grounded in the interstate commerce clause of the Constitution, supported this evolution. As national liquor regulations developed, they focused on the words that could be used to name a spirit based on how it was made not where it was made. And yet, the decades between American Independence and the beginning of the Industrial Revolution laid the foundation for the regional variations of bourbon and American whiskey we see today.

Rum: America's colonial spirit

Before the American Revolution, almost everything a person ate or drank in the British Colonies was local, except for rum. The Colonies in the Americas were part of a vast network of trade routes that extended from Europe to Africa, the Americas and back, known as the triangular trade. Europeans sold finished goods such as textiles and rum to Africa in exchange for slaves, the slaves were sold into forced labour in the Americas to produce tobacco, sugar cane, cotton and other raw materials, and those raw goods were sold to European manufacturers. However, instead of rum being produced in Europe, much of it was distilled in New England from molasses produced in the Caribbean. At that time, New England had hundreds of distilleries making and selling their rum throughout the Colonies and to traders bound for Africa. But once war broke out between the Colonies and Great Britain, the fire hose of molasses that flooded New England slowed to a trickle and made rum much more costly. After the war, lingering trade conflicts put rum out of reach for many Americans and instead they turned to locally made whiskey.

The Whiskey Rebellion

After ratification of the US Constitution in 1788 and the inauguration of George Washington in 1789, the new federal government flexed its increased taxing power to tackle the substantial debt load it had accumulated during the war. Secretary of the Treasury, Alexander Hamilton, proposed several ways for the government to raise cash, including duties on imported goods and an excise tax on US distilled spirits. And since whiskey consumption continued to grow year after year, Hamilton saw a great source of potential revenue. So, in the spring of 1791, Congress passed the tax and Washington sent out revenue men and inspectors to enforce its collection.

The tax quickly earned the ire of those on the frontier because it had to be paid in cash and some of its provisions favoured urban over rural distillers. Over the next three years, tensions grew from refusal to pay

Below: A tax collector tarred and feathered at Pigeon Creek, in Washington County, Pennsylvania, during the Whiskey Rebellion.

FAMOUS WHISKEY INSURRECTION IN PENNSYLVANIA.

to outright violence. Revenue collectors were turned away and a couple in Western Pennsylvania were even tarred and feathered by locals. Finally, in 1794, insurrection broke out when the federal government issued subpoenas for 60 Pennsylvania distillers who refused to pay the whiskey tax. Members of the Mingo Creek militia surrounded the house of General John Neville, a local politician and owner of a large distillery, who supported the federal marshal in delivering the subpoenas. Both sides exchanged gunfire, but when one of the militia leaders was shot during a ceasefire, the rebels set fire to the house and took Neville and a few other men prisoner. In response, President Washington sent three commissioners to negotiate with the whiskey rebels and at the same time called up a federal militia of almost 13,000 men, ultimately bringing the so-called Whiskey Rebellion to an end. But discontentment about the whiskey tax lingered and eventually coalesced into political support for Thomas Jefferson, who was elected president in 1800 and repealed the whiskey tax in 1802.

Geography shapes early American whiskey

But what type of whiskey were early Americans drinking? The answer has little to do with politics and more with geography. When Europeans first landed along the eastern coast of the Americas, they encountered

Algonquian-speaking tribes that by and large relied on seasonal hunting and gathering combined with part-time cultivation of beans, corn (maize) and winter squash, known as the Three Sisters. As settlers continued to arrive, they brought with them a wide variety of new animals and plants including wheat, rye, barley and oats.

The mix of grains that a farmer grew often depended on the geography and quality of the soil. Wheat requires better soil to thrive, so it is doubtful that any significant amount ever ended up in early American whiskey. Rye, on the other hand, grew well in poor soils up and down the east coast and had multiple uses. Corn was quickly adopted into the diets of European settlers in the Americas, and while it did not grow as successfully as rye on the east coast, its sweetness made it a good candidate for whiskey. Lastly, barley grows best in more northern latitudes and is the most common grain used to make beer. But even in the 18th century, distillers knew that a little bit of malted barley helped other grains ferment, although they did not understand the exact biochemistry.

Below: Mount Vernon, family home of President George Washington.

During the first century of the United States, this patchwork of commercial and geographic influences on grain production produced a few regional variations in American whiskey. Rye and corn grew well around the Chesapeake Bay, so it makes sense that when James Anderson opened a commercial distillery for George Washington at his Virginia plantation in the late 1790s, they made whiskey from a mixture of 60% rye, 35% corn and 5% malted barley. The Mount Vernon distillery is just across the Potomac River from Maryland and in the two years before Washington's death it sold double-distilled and quadruple-distilled whiskey. Over the decades that followed, the Maryland region became known for producing rye whiskey like Washington's,

THE WHISKEY CAPITAL OF THE WORLD

From 1837 to 1919, Peoria, Illinois boasted 24 breweries and 73 distilleries, and was touted as the 'whiskey capital of the world'. Peoria is situated about 160 miles (260km) south of Chicago on the Illinois River, and had an abundance of clean spring water and a network of rail and barge routes that brought Midwestern corn to its shores. These factors helped make Peoria a prime hub for distilling. In 1880, Peoria produced 18 million US gallons (68 million litres) of alcohol, more than the entire production of the state of Kentucky. The city reached its maximum production around 1894, with just six distilleries, owned by the Whiskey Trust, making 40 per cent of all the alcohol produced in the United States. All that liquor resulted in the Peoria tax district collecting about 21 per cent of the tax revenue for the entire country! Prohibition brought an abrupt end to Peoria's dominance, though it was partially revived in 1933 by Hiram Walker & Sons, owner of Canadian Club Whisky. Today, the city has only one active craft distillery just starting to make whiskey.

made with a good portion of corn in the mash to add sweetness. In contrast, the western Monongahela region of Pennsylvania became known for producing a spicier style of rye that contained little or no corn at all, since maize did not grow well in that area, whereas corn whiskey, balanced with a little rye for spice and malted barley for the benefit of the fermentation, became the dominant style in Kentucky and Tennessee due to the abundance of that staple crop. One commonality these early whiskeys had was that they were all drunk unaged, and the only reason to store them in oak barrels was for transportation.

Above: Peoria, Illinois, 1911.

Innovation shapes modern American whiskey

In the first half of the 19th century, a couple of important innovations began to change early American whiskey into what we know today. One of the challenges of any fermented food or beverage is ensuring that it develops in the desired way. A beer might ferment correctly and give you a great-tasting drink or it might go wrong and taste sour or spoiled. In the early 1800s, brewers and distillers did not know why these things happened but they developed strategies that increased consistency and success. It had been common practice for brewers to collect a portion of the foam that bubbled at the top of their vats and pitch it into the next batch of wort to brew into beer. In 1818, we find references to a distiller named Catherine Carpenter using a similar technique to sour her mashes that would prevent them from spoiling. Later in the 1830s, Dr James C Crow (see page 47), who studied chemistry and medicine at the University of Edinburgh, worked to improve the sour mash process and other

aspects of whiskey making by applying his scientific knowledge. It was also during this time that distillers and merchants noticed that whiskey stored for some time in charred barrels significantly improved in flavour and took on a pleasing colour, thus prompting the practice of purposefully storing whiskey in charred oak barrels for multiple years before its sale.

Rectifiers vs straight whiskey men

During the second half of the 19th century, American whiskey settled into two distinct styles known as straight whiskey and rectified whiskey, the former being the Kentucky bourbons, Tennessee whiskeys and Pennsylvania and Maryland rye whiskeys that were distilled and aged for many years. These whiskeys became sought after for their flavour and they were more expensive to make. However, enterprising businesses started looking for ways to cheat time and create a similar-tasting product for less money, thereby increasing their profit margin. This was rectified whiskey. In the 1880s and 1890s, the Distilling and Cattle Feeding

Company, also known as the Whiskey Trust, controlled as much as 80 per cent of all liquor production in the US. Rectifiers purchased unaged grain spirits from the Whiskey Trust, which was either blended with straight whiskey or simply adulterated before being sold to merchants. Distilling books of the time offered recipes for making rectified whiskey that might include benign ingredients like prune juice and tinctures made from wood or cloves to more dangerous additives such as iodine, tobacco juice and acids.

Unsurprisingly, many of the straight whiskey distillers were unhappy with how the rectifiers were abusing their spirits and, in their opinion, giving drinkers a vastly inferior product. In response, a group of distillers led by Colonel Edmund Haynes Taylor, Jr, began to petition the government for several protections. And with the help of US Secretary of the Treasury John G Carlisle, the straight whiskey distillers were able to get Congress to pass the Bottled-in-Bond Act of 1897. At that time, the law allowed distillers to hold their ageing barrels of whiskey or brandy in a bonded warehouse tax free until it was bottled and sold. The law stipulated that any aged spirits bottled under its provisions had to be of the same type (bourbon, rye, brandy and so on), aged for a minimum of four years, distilled in the same season and reduced in strength only with pure water to 100 proof (50% ABV). The law also mandated that an agent of the Treasury would stay on site with the keys to the warehouse to control the movement of whiskey, collect all appropriate taxes and ensure that the vatting and proofing of spirits adhered to all the provisions of the law before bottling. Once bottled, the whiskey would be sealed with a federal strip stamp, thereby making it a federal crime to tamper with the bottle or the whiskey inside. In addition, the law also required that the bottle be clearly marked with the name of the distillery, the season and year it was distilled and when it was bottled.

The Bottled-in-Bond Act provided straight whiskey distillers with some legal protection from adulteration by rectifiers, and it was also the first ever consumer protection law in the United States. For drinkers, the law meant that when they purchased bottled-in-bond whiskey

Above: Colonel Edmund Haynes Taylor, Jr.

Above: Vintage label for a bottle of 'Old Kentucky General' bourbon whiskey, 1955.

Whiskey held This MAN Too Long Now The "WEAK" MUST Support The "STRONG"

Suffrage-Series-No.4

Above: A Temperance postcard from Edith Parsons Williams's 1912 New York Suffragettes Series, No. 4: 'Whiskey held this man too long now the "weak" must support the "strong".'

Below: Local police dumping barrels of beer seized from a train in Scranton, Pennsylvania, during Prohibition.

or brandy, the US federal government gave its guarantee that the spirit in the bottle was exactly as labelled. And over time, bottled-in-bond spirits became the benchmark for quality and authenticity that drinkers looked for.

At the turn of the 20th century, the public had become genuinely concerned about the quality and healthfulness of the goods they were buying, including whiskey. The government began to study the question of what makes whiskey unique, and looked for measurable standards that could be enforced. After much political wrangling, President William Howard Taft created a system for defining straight whiskey, blended whiskey and imitation whiskey that he believed balanced the interests of distillers, rectifiers and the public. Straight whiskey was now defined as a spirit made from a fermented mash of grains, distilled between 140 and 160 proof (70–80% ABV) and aged in charred oak barrels.

But the Taft Decision, as it was known, was short-lived, and just ten years later, Temperance crusaders succeeded in ratifying the 18th Amendment to the Constitution prohibiting the manufacture, transportation or sale of alcohol.

Defining American whiskey post-Prohibition

After 13 years of the so-called noble experiment, National Prohibition was repealed with the ratification of the 21st Amendment and the government went to work rewriting the nation's liquor laws. In 1935, the new Federal Alcohol Administration resurrected the Taft Decision and added a couple of additional elements, largely creating the definitions that the federal government uses today. The new standards of identity defined bourbon as a whiskey made from a fermented mash of not less than 51% corn, distilled to not more than 160 proof (80% ABV) and barrelled at not more than 110 proof (55% ABV) in charred oak barrels. Rye whiskey followed the same pattern except that it required a minimum of 51% rye grain in the mash. Three years later, the government added the requirement that bourbon, rye and other similar whiskeys must rest in charred *new* oak barrels, to help keep coopers employed during the Great Depression. Additionally, the government defined straight whiskey as any whiskey such as bourbon or rye that was stored in a charred new oak barrel for at least 24 months and bottled at no less than 80 proof (40% ABV). Lastly, as with the Taft Decision before it, the new standards of identity allowed all types of liquor to be made in any state in the country.

The rise and fall of American whiskey

In the years that followed the repeal of Prohibition and World War II, distillers took advantage of the fact that there were no regional restrictions on what types of whiskey they could make. However, while one is sure to find examples of rye whiskey from Kentucky or bourbon from Pennsylvania, the most popular brands of each style came from the same states that made them famous in the 19th century. But as the American post-war economy boomed in the 1950s and 1960s, more and more whiskey drinkers were buying bourbon or Canadian whisky (which had gained popularity during Prohibition) and sales of American rye whiskey began to lag.

But even the popularity of bourbon would not last. In 1967, Kentucky bourbon production peaked when the state's distillers laid down 1.9 million barrels, and that

Above: A vintage advertisement for Sugar Bowl Straight Bourbon Whiskey.

number would gradually slide to less than 1 million barrels by 1974, due to a generational shift in drinking habits. In the 1970s, bourbon and rye became the spirits that your parents drank, while vodka and to a lesser extent tequila were the newer hip spirits.

As the 1970s ended and the American whiskey industry struggled to compete, the last remaining rye distillers in Maryland and Pennsylvania closed their doors. By the mid-1980s, the last remaining barrels of the old-style ryes were used up and the near two-hundred-year history of Pennsylvania and Maryland-style rye whiskeys ended.

A new hope

At the same time that big whiskey was consolidating and struggling to survive, craft distilling was quietly beginning out West. Three distillers, Jörg Rupf from Germany, Hubert Germain-Robin from France and Stephen McCarthy from Oregon (see page 209), began making European-inspired brandies on the West Coast from locally grown fruit. Then in 1993, Fritz Maytag, owner of San Francisco's Anchor Brewing Company, founded Anchor Distilling and began making rye whiskey shortly thereafter. Looking all the way back to early American whiskey for inspiration, Maytag and his distiller, Bruce Joseph, started ageing two types of

Right: Fritz Maytag, former owner of San Francisco's Anchor Brewing and Anchor Distilling.

whiskey made from 100% malted rye, one aged in toasted barrels and the other in charred new oak barrels. Little by little the idea of craft whiskey spread throughout the country as people sought inspiration from family and local history, as well as the surrounding agriculture.

The rediscovery of great American whiskeys from Kentucky, Tennessee and Indiana has coincided with a growing interest in local and craft distilled whiskeys. These two factors have helped to spark renewed interest in near-forgotten styles and drive enthusiasm for new regional ones such as Missouri bourbon, Empire Rye and Pacific Northwest American single malt whiskey to name just a few.

Today, the quality and diversity of American whiskey have never been greater. The story of American whiskey in the 21st century is not just about Kentucky and Tennessee. Every state in the Union is experimenting, creating and writing its own chapter. What follows on these pages is by no means exhaustive but a snapshot of the regional diversity of bourbon and American whiskey available today.

Above: A distiller measuring proof at Westland Distillery in Seattle, Washington (see page 213).

What is American whiskey?

Over the past two hundred years and across the globe, whisky generally has come to mean a grain spirit that is purposefully stored in a wooden barrel before being drunk. But how one gets to that result has varied country by country, and region by region, giving fans of whisky a huge palette of aromas and flavours to enjoy. In that time, American whiskey has taken its place among the great styles of the world and stands out from the rest largely due to a combination of mixed grain mash bills, new charred oak barrels and the climate in which the barrels age.

Mash bills

The term mash bill simply refers to the types of grains used to make a whiskey and their ratios, and in the late 18th century, when regional differences in American whiskey were beginning to form, geography and economics played a significant role in determining the mash bill. Many farm distillers made whiskey from the

Opposite: An oak barrel being charred at Kelvin Cooperage in Louisville, Kentucky.

BOURBON is required by US law to be made with a minimum of 51% corn, though in practice most are made with 60–80% corn, plus one flavouring grain and some malted barley for the enzymes necessary for fermentation. Rye is the most common flavouring grain, and it can make up anywhere between 10% and 35% of the mash. Wheat is the second most commonly used flavouring grain and may account for 10–20% of the mash. Rye and wheat are referred to as flavouring grains because once corn whiskey ages in a barrel for a couple of years it will lose much of its original character. Lastly, there are a small but significant number of four-grain bourbons that are usually made from a mash of corn, rye, wheat and malted barley.

RYE WHISKEY requires a minimum of 51% rye. After the closure of the last Pennsylvania and Maryland distillers in the early 1980s, the only rye whiskeys on the market were distilled in Kentucky and these were made from the minimum mash of 51% rye. Today, however, some of the bestselling ryes are made from a mash of 95% rye and 5% malted barley, with many others well above 60% rye, as they were back in George Washington's day.

WHEAT WHISKEY requires a minimum of 51% wheat. For many years, the only wheat whiskey widely available was Bernheim Original

Kentucky Straight Wheat Whiskey, which was made from a mash of 51% wheat, 37% corn and 12% malted barley. However, there are several craft distillers now making fantastic whiskey from 100% wheat.

MALT WHISKEY is required by US law to be made with a minimum of 51% malted grains. The malt can be malted barley, malted rye, malted wheat or even malted corn combined with up to 49% other raw grains. For nearly a decade, you could find both 51% malt whiskeys made in Kentucky by the heritage distillers and 100% malted barley whiskeys from craft distillers. Today, though, many of the craft distillers refer to their 100% malt whiskey as American single malt.

AMERICAN SINGLE MALT WHISKEY (ASMW) at the time of writing is not yet a legally defined term. Several groups have petitioned the government to create a standard for ASMW, which among other things require it be made from 100% malted barley. Here the term single refers to the fact that the whiskey comes from a single distillery, not the use of one type of grain. While it is common in Scotland and other single malt-producing countries to only use distillers' malt in their whiskey, many US distillers use a combination of distillers' malt and speciality malts that introduce additional flavours to the mash and the resulting whiskey.

| Corn (maize) | Barley | Rye | Wheat |

remaining grains they could not eat themselves or sell in the local market. Consequently, early American whiskey styles can be thought of more as field blends than recipes designed to produce a specific flavour. However, commercial distillers removed from the economics of market farming used the mash bill as one way to differentiate their whiskey from that of their competitors.

Barrels

For the core styles of American whiskey, bourbon, rye, wheat and malt whiskeys, US law requires that they must be stored at not more than 125 proof (62.5% ABV) in charred new oak containers – another element that contributes to their unique flavour. As barrels are being shaped, coopers use small fires to heat the wood, allowing it to be bent into shape. During this process, the wood is toasted, which begins the process of degrading the surface of the barrel and breaking down tannins and other compounds in the wood – all of which will bring flavour to the whiskey. After toasting, the inside of the barrel is allowed to catch fire. The longer the barrel burns, the deeper the char eats into the wood, and the depth is described in numbers, with No. 1 char lasting just 15 seconds and No. 4 char lasting 55–60 seconds. While distillers are free to use any char they want, No. 3 and No. 4 chars are the most common.

Storage conditions

The conditions in which barrels are stored have a significant impact on the flavour and character of the whiskey as it matures. In Kentucky, it is common to find warehouses dedicated to ageing whiskey barrels known as rickhouses. Many of them are large wooden structures, multiple storeys tall and clad in tin without temperature controls. In this type of rickhouse, you end up with temperature and humidity gradients within the building that rise and fall with the seasons. The consequence of ageing whiskey barrels in this sort of building is that the top floors are hotter than the bottom, and southern-facing walls get more heat than northern ones. Both the alcohol and water increase or decrease in volume as they are heated or cooled by diurnal and seasonal changes in temperature. This causes the whiskey to push into and pull out of the wood and is part of the maturation process. Some distillers prefer instead to store their barrels in other types of warehouses that may be made of brick or concrete, which can slow the impact of diurnal changes in temperature. There are also distillers such as Michter's that control the temperature by the use of air conditioners in the summer and/or heaters in the winter; they see temperature as just one more variable to control during the ageing process to produce whiskey as they want it to taste.

Just like with cooking that can be slow and low or fast and hot, lower ambient temperatures will cause slower flavour extraction from the barrel, whereas higher ambient temperatures in the ageing warehouse will result in the whiskey maturing more quickly. But because the United States is so big, it has many different climates that impact on the regional character of American whiskey. For example, whiskeys aged in the temperate Pacific Northwest near the Pacific Ocean will mature differently from barrels stored in the hot and dry climate of the Texas Hill Country. And even though most American whiskey is made in Kentucky, Tennessee and Indiana, the proliferation of whiskey distilleries around the country now allows us to taste the impact of climate on aged whiskey, which was not possible 20 years ago.

Above: A cooper assembles white oak staves into a barrel at the Brown-Forman Corporation cooperage facility in Louisville, Kentucky.

Opposite: Wooden ricks holding barrels of whiskey in Lynchburg, Tennessee.

General mash bill terms

When a specific mash bill is not provided in the whiskey profiles under the featured distilleries, the following terms are used to give a general sense of the mix of grains in a whiskey.

BOURBON

Rye boubon mash: corn, rye (18% or less), malted barley

High-rye bourbon mash: corn, rye (more than 18%), malted barley

Wheated bourbon mash: corn, wheat (35% or less), malted barley

Four-grain bourbon mash: corn, rye, wheat, malted barley

RYE

Maryland rye mash: two-thirds rye, one-third other grains, usually corn and malted barley

Pennsylvania rye mash: 75% rye (may include malted rye), 25% malted barley, sometimes wheat

Empire Rye mash: Minimum 75% New York-grown rye, no more than 25% other grains

Kentucky
Bourbon

Kentucky bourbon is the king of American whiskey. While it is true that whiskey made from rye was the first major whiskey style to fill the glasses of Americans, Congress was right to name bourbon as 'America's Native Spirit' in 2007, when it declared September to be National Bourbon Heritage month. Born during the westward push from the original 13 states, it is made primarily from North America's native corn (maize), and aged in charred barrels of American white oak. For much of its history, Kentucky bourbon has been prized for its signature character and has seen countless imitations and attempts to shortcut its simple recipe of grain, water, yeast, oak and time.

The story of this now global phenomenon is filled with men and women who endeavoured to make the finest whiskey they could and share it in its pure state, without additives. Slowly, this group of committed bourbon distillers realized their dream, despite a political movement aimed at killing their business, world wars and

Opposite: A beautiful evening scene in Kentucky's Bluegrass region.

Climatic conditions: Louisville, KY – 16 active distilleries

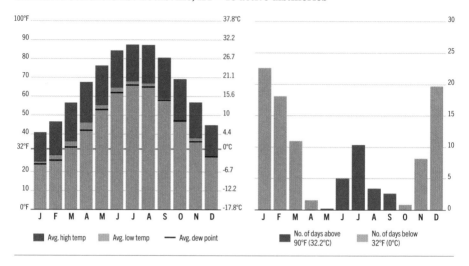

Avg. high temp   Avg. low temp   — Avg. dew point

No. of days above 90°F (32.2°C)   No. of days below 32°F (0°C)

a depression in the global economy. Kentucky straight bourbon whiskey reached its zenith around Congress's 1964 declaration, only to be undone by a generational shift in drinking preferences that persisted for nearly three decades. However, in the late 1990s and early 2000s, another cultural, economic and palate shift was underway that led many drinkers to recognize that Kentucky straight bourbon is one of the world's great whiskeys.

History

By the time Daniel Boone and other early American frontiersmen arrived in Kentucky in the latter half of the 18th century, it was sparsely inhabited by a few American

Above: Antique botanical illustration of corn (maize).

Region Name:	Commonwealth of Kentucky
Nickname:	The Bluegrass State
Capital City:	Frankfort
Population:	4,467,673
Number of Active Distilleries:	95
Whiskey Fact:	Kentucky has 9.1 million barrels of ageing whiskey or 2 barrels for every person living in the state.

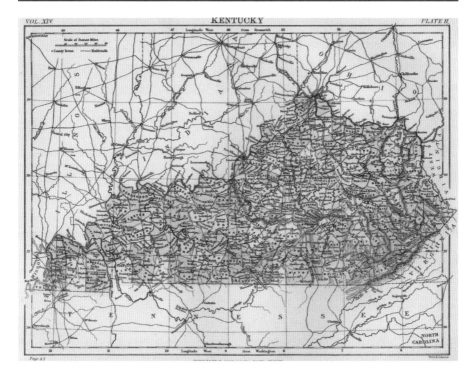

Indian tribes including the Shawnee from Ohio, as well as the Chickasaw, and Cherokee from Tennessee. Soon after the US Declaration of Independence in 1776, the Virginia General Assembly claimed the Kentucky region to their west and designated it as a new county under their jurisdiction. Not long after, settlers started pouring into Kentucky both through the Cumberland Gap in the south and via the Ohio River in the north. By 1785, the region had been divided into various counties, including Bourbon County, named in honour of the French Royal House of Bourbon, who aided the US in her struggle for independence. On 1 June 1792, the new federal government admitted Kentucky as the 15th state in the Union.

As with the Shawnee and Cherokee before them, American settlers relied on corn (maize) as a staple crop, since it grew abundantly and was known by farm distillers to make a sweet whiskey. And as with other types of early American whiskey, this corn whiskey was

Above: An official map of the state of Kentucky, drawn in 1898.

probably distilled by rural farmers from excess grain into whiskey that served as a medicine, analgesic, celebratory drink and medium of exchange. However, less than 30 years after statehood, there is evidence that bourbon whiskey had become a commercial spirit, distilled from a sour mash of corn and other grains, and purposefully stored in charred barrels to mellow the whiskey and add flavour. By the 1850s, Kentucky bourbon was growing in popularity, spread in part by influential figures like US Senator Henry Clay. Barrels of old bourbon were carried overland throughout the southeast and on river boats down to New Orleans where barrels made their way to metropolitan centres along the Gulf and east coasts.

The popularity of straight bourbon whiskey was on the rise across the country, but with the start of the American Civil War in 1861, it would experience nearly a century of stops and starts in production. As a border state between the North and South, the citizens of Kentucky had divided loyalties, with about 100,000 Kentuckians fighting for the Union and about 40,000 for the Confederacy. One of the lasting consequences of this was the loss of manpower for many of the small farm and commercial distilleries that dotted the state, leaving only a few large distillers active. In addition, areas controlled by the Confederacy officially prohibited the production of whiskey and brandy, requiring the crops and materials involved for use in the war.

Post-Civil War, whiskey in America boomed, but Temperance, state prohibition and a world war would bring it to a stop. In the 1880s and 1890s, considerable volumes of both rectified and straight whiskey (see page 18) were being consumed during the first golden age of the cocktail. However, the Temperance message urging individuals to moderate their drinking had a dramatic impact on the per capita consumption of alcohol, driving it down to levels equivalent to what we see today. That message gradually morphed into outright prohibition and drove several states, including Tennessee, to outlaw the production and sale of liquor.

Meanwhile, Europe was headed for war. After suffering attacks by German U-boats, the US was unable to stay out of the conflict and it officially declared war

Above: Advertising label for Bininger's Old Kentucky Bourbon, 1860.

on Germany on 2 April 1917. As part of the war effort, the federal government required distillers to shift production from whiskey and other spirits to industrial alcohol that was used to make munitions, while a proposed amendment to the Constitution prohibiting the production, distribution and sale of alcohol was working its way through Congress. The proposed amendment was presented to the states for ratification on 18 December 1917, World War I came to an end on 11 November 1918 and National Prohibition became law on 16 January 1919, coming into effect a year later. In Kentucky at the time of Prohibition, the state had about 183 operating distilleries, but by 1920 that number had shrunk to 4.

A handful of distilleries applied for a licence to sell medicinal liquor and six were approved by the federal government, four of them in Kentucky: A. Ph. Stitzel Distillery, Brown-Forman, O.F.C. Distillery (today's Buffalo Trace Distillery) and Glenmore Distillery. In the first year alone, the six licensed distilleries sold about 8 million US gallons (30 million litres) of medicinal alcohol, which led to a crackdown on the number of prescriptions a doctor could prescribe. By 1926, the stock of medicinal spirits was so low that Assistant Secretary of the Treasury Lincoln Andrews warned that the country would run out if production did not begin again. Finally, in 1929, Congress authorized the production of

Above: A vintage advertisement for Old Pepper whiskey, from the 1890s.

Left: Last call at a tavern in Covington, Kentucky on the day before Prohibition was ratified, 1919.

2 million US gallons (7.5 million litres) of whiskey annually, split 70 per cent for bourbon and 30 per cent for rye whiskey. But despite this new authorization, only A. Ph. Stitzel Distillery and Brown-Forman began distilling whiskey again, due in part to a lack of trained personnel and equipment (some of which had been sold for scrap).

The October 1929 stock market crash and resulting Great Depression decimated huge swathes of the US economy, but Prohibition's repeal would see significant reinvestment in the future of Kentucky bourbon. On 5 December 1933, the 21st Amendment to the US Constitution officially repealed the 18th Amendment, ending Prohibition, and shortly thereafter, several members of the extensive Beam family began working to get back to making bourbon. The 70-year-old James 'Jim' Beauregard Beam quickly found two investors from Chicago and they worked to build a new distillery, filling their first barrels in 1935. That same year, President Franklin Roosevelt signed the Federal Alcohol Administration Act, which created the new legal framework for distilled spirits and contained the production requirements for a whiskey to be labelled as bourbon. With a couple of exceptions, it is the same standard of identity used for bourbon today. At the same time that Jim Beam was rebuilding his distillery, his cousin Joseph L Beam approached the Shapira family, who had successfully built up a chain of department stores during the Great Depression, to help fund his vision for a new distillery. With the help of two other local investors, they purchased land and built a new distillery, and at the end of 1935 they too began filling barrels. The Shapiras needed cash flow to keep the distillery running, so they began with selling young whiskey, then moved to a two-year-old brand called Bourbon Falls and at the end of 1939 debuted their Old Heaven Hill Bottled-In-Bond Kentucky Bourbon, which quickly became a bestseller. But in those four short years, it was also clear that another massive war was brewing. And after the Imperial Japanese Navy Air Service attacked Pearl Harbor on 7 December 1941, US distillers were called upon to produce industrial alcohol for the war effort.

Above: The Jim Beam Distillery in Clermont, Kentucky.

After nearly four bloody years of fighting, the US had a booming industrial war economy that was able to transition to a booming industrial consumer economy that had many thirsty Americans looking to Kentucky bourbon to fill their glass. In the post-war era of the 1950s and 1960s, sales of brands like Old Crow and Jim Beam (see page 52) dominated the whiskey business, and Kentucky bourbon distillers were laying down over one million new barrels every year in anticipation that sales would continue to grow. It was at this time, in 1964, that Congress declared that bourbon whiskey 'is a distinctive product of the United States and is unlike other types of alcoholic beverage'. But the good times did not last.

By the end of the 1960s, the writing was on the wall and bourbon sales began a steep fall. This time bourbon's troubles were not caused by war or new legislation but by the individual choices of a new generation that no longer wanted the same old spirits their parents and grandparents drank. For three solid decades, production and the number of Kentucky bourbon barrels stored throughout the state were in decline. These same distillers attempted to draw back drinkers who had moved on to Canadian whiskey and

Above: Two vintage advertisements for Kentucky Straight Bourbon Whiskey from the 1950s.

vodka with the release of new brands of blended American whiskey, light whiskey and spirit whiskey. It was also at this time that Jim Beam Kentucky Bourbon lost its position as the number one selling brand of straight whiskey, supplanted by Jack Daniel's Tennessee Whiskey, which still holds the lead position to this day.

The year 1999 was another inflection point for Kentucky bourbon when barrel inventories began to climb as sales improved, and have not stopped yet. In the late 1980s and early 1990s, Kentucky distillers began offering single-barrel, extra-aged and cask-strength expressions of bourbon that, along with a cocktail revival, helped drive more consumer interest in offerings from the Bluegrass State. But there was so much whiskey that significant numbers of what were then non-distiller brands like Angel's Envy, Bulleit Bourbon (see page 123) and Michter's were purchasing bulk whiskey or contracting other distillers to bottle whiskey for them with great success. And it was not long before enterprising craft distillers started presenting a new take on a classic American whiskey. Today, Kentucky bourbon is more popular than it ever was in the past, and both old and new distilleries are offering incredible quality at every price point. The dizzying array of Kentucky bourbons on the market is in part testament to how this regional style of whiskey has captivated the American imagination.

Production requirements

All bourbon made in Kentucky must adhere to the federal definition specified in the Standards of Identity for Distilled Spirits, in that it must be fermented from a mash of grains that consists of at least 51% corn, distilled no higher than 160 proof (80% ABV) and stored in a charred new oak barrel at no higher than 125 proof (62.5% ABV). Absent from these regulations is any specified duration for storing the whiskey in the barrel for it to be called bourbon. However, the Commonwealth of Kentucky also requires that any whiskey produced in the state that bears the state's name on the label must have been aged a minimum of one full year, except for corn whiskey, which can be bottled unaged. Therefore, any bourbon or rye

Above: White oak bourbon barrels being constructed at Kelvin Cooperage in Louisville, Kentucky.

whiskey, and so on, produced and aged at least one year in the state can be called Kentucky bourbon and so on, but any non-corn whiskey aged less than one year cannot.

The law was written around 1936 and since then there have been a few small tweaks to the wording. The last update, which came in 2017, elaborated on the word 'produced' to mean that the whiskey had to be made from grains that were cooked, fermented and distilled in the state. There is some speculation that the legislature wanted to pre-empt any outside company trading on the good name of Kentucky bourbon by distilling new make whiskey in another state, then ageing it for at least a year in state and selling it as Kentucky whiskey. Back in 2014, Diageo admitted in court that they had transferred some 16,000 barrels of whiskey distilled in Tennessee and stored them at a facility in Louisville, Kentucky because they had maxed out warehouse storage and were in the process of building more rickhouses. However, there was also no evidence that any of that whiskey went into spirits labelled Kentucky whiskey. So, in the end, consumers can rest assured that any whiskey labelled Kentucky bourbon is well protected by both federal and state law.

Above: Bottling, at Old Pepper Distillery, Lexington, Kentucky.

KENTUCKY BOURBON
distilleries to try

NORTHERN KENTUCKY

Neeley Family Distillery

Sparta, KY 38° 42' 24.6" N, 84° 56' 41.5" W

In 2015, Roy and son Royce Neeley ended more than ten generations of Kentucky moonshining with the founding of their Neeley Family Distillery. Roy built the distillery, while Royce serves as the head distiller. Carrying on the family legacy, Royce ferments a sweet wheated bourbon mash in open cypress fermenters, before being triple pot distilled and aged in 53-US-gallon (200-litre) charred new oak barrels. In addition to bourbon, the Neeleys also make moonshine and a few flavoured whiskeys.

WHISKEYS

MASH BILL: 64% CORN, 28% WHEAT, 8% MALTED BARLEY

Neeley Family Distillery Kentucky Single Barrel Bourbon Whiskey Barrel Strength ABV varies

Above: Neeley Family Distillery Kentucky Single Barrel Bourbon Whiskey.

IF YOU TRY ONE...
Neeley Family Distillery Kentucky Single Barrel Bourbon Whiskey
52% ABV (104 proof)

With a lovely aroma of spiced red wine, oak and cloves, on the tongue, it explodes with sweet notes of vanilla and cream, followed by a healthy dose of green oak. On the finish, there are light flavours of sweet apple, vanilla, tobacco, toasted wood and lemon pith. While the aroma is utterly captivating, it still tastes a bit young. Over time, these green flavours are sure to mature and develop, creating a more complex spirit. Even at 54% ABV there is very little heat, testament to the care with which the whiskey was distilled. But in the meantime, it will make a great Old-Fashioned.

Bluegrass Distillers

Lexington, KY 38° 03' 35.3" N, 84° 29' 30.1" W

Entrepreneurs Sam Rock and Nathan Brown based in Lexington, looking to move into the distilling business, founded Bluegrass Distillers in 2012, and hired head distiller Kee Pyle to create their mash bills and oversee production from mashing to bottling. Pyle has created three core bourbon mash bills: a high-rye, a wheated and a wheated bourbon mash with blue corn. Bluegrass also partners with a couple of cider makers, lending them their used bourbon barrels to age their cider and then using those cider-soaked barrels to finish their two-year-old wheated bourbon.

WHISKEYS

MASH BILL: 75% YELLOW CORN, 21% RYE, 4% MALTED BARLEY

Bluegrass Distillers High Rye Kentucky Straight Bourbon Whiskey 45% ABV (90 proof)

Below: Bluegrass Distillers Blue Corn Kentucky Straight Bourbon Whiskey.

MASH BILL: 80% YELLOW CORN, 20% RYE

Bluegrass Distillers High Rye Bottled-in-Bond Kentucky Straight Bourbon Whiskey 50% ABV (100 proof)

MASH BILL: 75% YELLOW CORN, 21% WHEAT, 4% MALTED BARLEY

Bluegrass Distillers Kentucky Straight Bourbon Whiskey
– **Wheated** 45% ABV (90 proof)
– **Wheated Finished in Hard Cider Barrels** 45% ABV (90 proof)

MASH BILL: 75% BLUE CORN, 21% WHEAT, 4% MALTED BARLEY

Bluegrass Distillers Blue Corn Kentucky Straight Bourbon Whiskey 45% ABV (90 proof)

IF YOU TRY ONE...

Bluegrass Distillers Blue Corn Kentucky Straight Bourbon Whiskey 45% ABV (90 proof)

A rich aroma of dried dates, milk chocolate, peach skins and baking spices heavy on the nutmeg, and a light touch of buttery Chardonnay. On the palate, there is a strong flavour of butterscotch, cinnamon and vanilla, and while there is not a distinct oak flavour, its presence is felt, since the whiskey is well balanced between sweet and dry spice. On the finish, the woodiness increases with rich notes of caramel and vanilla floating in the background. It is very complex and richly flavoured for such a young whiskey. For those who have a bit of a sweet tooth but do not want a whiskey with added sugar, this blue corn bourbon will hit the spot.

Old Pepper Distillery

Lexington, KY 38° 03' 24.1" N 84° 31' 11.3" W

In 1878, James E Pepper and George Starkweather purchased the old Henry Clay distillery in Fayette County, Kentucky. One year earlier, Pepper had to declare bankruptcy and the Old Oscar Pepper Distillery, which his father had built, passed from Colonel E H Taylor, Jr to George T Stagg, and finally to Labrot and Graham (see page 47). But with Starkweather's investment, Pepper was able to build a modern (by 1880s standards) distillery that could produce 23 barrels of whiskey a day.

Their primary brands were Old Pepper Whiskey and Old Henry Clay Rye Whiskey. Business boomed and made both men very wealthy until an economic depression hit in 1893 and the distillery was placed in receivership three years later. However, at the auction for the distillery, the only bidder was Pepper's wife Ella Offutt Pepper with money earned from her prize-winning racehorses. Using a series of legal filings, James was able to regain control of the distillery and production resumed until his death in 1906. Mrs Pepper sold the distillery to a group of Chicago investors, who ran the company through Prohibition, selling Old Pepper as licensed medicinal whiskey. In 1933, the distillery caught fire and burned down and was rebuilt a year later by its new owner Schenley Products, which ran the distillery until 1958 when it closed. Five decades passed and the legacy of Old Pepper was revived by Amir Peay, an entrepreneur from Washington DC who began by selling sourced whiskey and in 2016 started rebuilding the Pepper distillery. A year later, the revived distillery filled its first barrel of whiskey in almost 60 years. In addition to bourbon, Peay also sells James E. Pepper 1776 Straight Rye Whiskey, Old Pepper Straight Rye Whiskey Single Barrel, and Old Henry Clay

Above: Old Pepper Distillery, Lexington, Kentucky.

Straight Rye Whiskey. The rye for these whiskeys was originally sourced from MGP Distillery in Lawrenceburg, IN (see page 125) though, in 2021, their own Lexington-distilled and aged rye will be mature enough to begin blending with sourced rye, presumably with the goal of transitioning to all in-house whiskey.

WHISKEYS

MASH BILL: 60% CORN, 36% RYE, 4% MALTED BARLEY

James E. Pepper 1776 Straight Bourbon Whiskey 50% ABV (100 proof)

Above: James E. Pepper 1776 Straight Bourbon Whiskey.

IF YOU TRY ONE...

James E. Pepper 1776 Straight Bourbon Whiskey
50% ABV (100 proof)

The aroma overall is light with notes of oak and just a faint hint of sweetened cherry. On the palate, there is a stronger taste of oak, sweet tea and more distant flavours of underripe peach and cream with a touch of vanilla. On the finish, there are soft notes of oak, sweet cherries, toffee and vanilla. At just over three years old, this is a nice wood-forward bourbon that will work on the rocks or in any classic cocktail, such as a Mint Julep (see page 62).

Woodford Reserve Distillery

Versailles, KY 38° 06' 47.1" N, 84° 48' 45.4" W

The history of the Woodford Reserve Distillery begins with Elijah Pepper who was born in Fauquier County, Virginia around the time of the American Revolution. In 1797, Pepper moved to Woodford County, Kentucky with his wife and brother-in-law where he built a distillery. After a short spell in Bourbon County, the Peppers returned to Woodford County around 1812 and purchased 200 acres (81 hectares) on Glenn's Creek and built a farm, gristmill and distillery. When Pepper died in 1831, his 350-acre (142-hectare) estate, which he willed to his wife Sarah, included 6 copper stills, 74 mash tubs, 41 barrels of ageing whiskey, 290 animals and 25 slaves, who they continued to own until the end of the Civil War. In 1838, Sarah sold the distillery to her son Oscar Pepper who replaced the log buildings with larger ones built from limestone. It was at this time that Pepper hired the Scottish chemist Dr James C Crow to work for him, and made both Old Pepper and Old Crow bourbons. By 1878, the Old Pepper Distillery was owned by Labrot and Graham, who renovated the distillery in 1895 and ran it until Prohibition. After it had changed hands various times, Brown-Forman, one of the previous owners, repurchased the distillery and installed three Scottish pot stills. It was renamed the Woodford Reserve Distillery in 1996 with the launch of Woodford Reserve Bourbon.

WHISKEYS

MASH BILL: 72% CORN, 18% RYE, 10% MALTED BARLEY

Woodford Reserve Kentucky Straight Bourbon Whiskey
– **Original** 45.2% ABV (90.4 proof)
– **Double Oaked** 45.2% ABV (90.4 proof)
– **Distiller's Select Kentucky Derby®** 45.2% ABV (90.4 proof)
– **Baccarat Edition** 45.2% ABV (90.4 proof) Finished in XO Cognac barrels.

Below: Woodford Reserve Distillery, Versailles, Kentucky.

Above: Woodford Reserve Kentucky Straight Bourbon Whiskey.

CENTRAL KENTUCKY

Heaven Hill Distillery, Bernheim Facility

Louisville, KY 38° 14' 41.4" N, 85° 46' 53.5" W

Isaac Bernheim emigrated from Germany in 1867 and ended up in Paducah, Kentucky working for a liquor wholesaler, eventually opening his own liquor business with his brother Bernard. By April 1897, they had opened their new Bernheim Distillery in Louisville, and became known for making wheated bourbon and selling it under a couple of brands including I.W. Harper. During Prohibition, the Bernheims were able to continue selling their spirits as medicinal whiskey, but after nearly 40 years in business, Bernheim sold the distillery to a group of Chicago businessmen, who sold it on four years later to the Schenley Distillers Corporation. By the 1990s, the Bernheim Distillery was owned by United Distillers, the precursor to Diageo, who tore down the old distillery and rebuilt a new one in its place in 1992. But due to slow bourbon sales, United did not use the distillery fully. Finally, in 1999, Heaven Hill purchased the distillery and renovated it to meet their needs after a fire three years earlier destroyed their Bardstown distillery. Over the years, Heaven Hill has continued to expand the production facility and in 2017, after a $25 million investment, Bernheim became the largest single site producer of Kentucky bourbon in the United States, with an annual capacity of over 400,000 barrels.

WHISKEYS

MASH BILL: 68% CORN, 20% WHEAT, 12% MALTED BARLEY

Larceny Kentucky Straight Bourbon Whiskey
– **Small Batch** 46% ABV (92 proof)
– **Barrel Proof** ABV varies

Old Fitzgerald Bottled-in-Bond Kentucky Straight Bourbon Whiskey 50% ABV (100 proof)
– **Green Label Spring Release Age varies**
– **Black Label Fall Release Age varies**
– **Red Label Distillery Edition 14 Years Old**

IF YOU TRY ONE...

Larceny Kentucky Straight Bourbon Whiskey
Small Batch 46% ABV (92 proof)

On the nose, there is a strong aroma of oak and cedar, with notes of tobacco, leather and sweet cherries. The flavour is full of spicy nutmeg and clove, with hints of candied orange and milk chocolate. A very woody bourbon with strong oak tannins and a touch of heat that starts in the mouth and travels down your chest. The finish lingers with powerful wood and spice notes, with a bit of residual heat from the alcohol. This will make a good Manhattan, emphasizing the baking spice and wood notes. For those who enjoy oak-forward bourbons, Larceny is a solid purchase.

Above: Larceny Kentucky Straight Bourbon Whiskey Small Batch.

Four Roses Distillery

Lawrenceburg, KY 37° 58' 25.0" N, 84° 53' 51.7" W

The Four Roses Distillery as it exists today was built in 1910 by J T S Brown and his son Creel Brown, brother and nephew to George Brown, co-founder of Brown-Forman. J T S Brown purchased the distillery in 1894, which, according to some accounts, had had a distilling operation on site since 1818. The distillery closed in 1917

in the lead-up to Prohibition and was refurbished in 1933 after its repeal. About a decade later, Seagram purchased the distillery and moved production of Four Roses to Lawrenceburg from its earlier home at the Frankfort Distilling Co. After the dissolution of Seagram in the early 2000s, Kirin Brewery Company purchased the distillery. Four Roses is unique in that they distil and age ten separate bourbons using two mash bills and five yeast strains. Each whiskey in their portfolio is made from one or more of these bourbons to create a specific bourbon profile. Four Roses uses a four-letter code to track each bourbon where O stands for Old Prentice, S for Straight Whiskey, V, K, O, Q and F are yeasts, B is a mash bill of 60% corn, 35% rye and 5% malted barley, and E is a mash bill of 75% corn, 20% rye and 5% malted barley.

WHISKEYS

MASH BILL: OBSV, OBSK, OBSO, OBSQ, OBSF, OESV, OESK, OESO, OESQ, OESF

Four Roses Yellow Label Kentucky Straight Bourbon Whiskey
40% ABV (80 proof)

MASH BILL: OBSK, OBSO, OESK, OESO

Four Roses Small Batch Kentucky Straight Bourbon Whiskey
45% ABV (90 proof)

MASH BILL: OBSV, OBSK, OBSF, OESV, OESK, OESF

Four Roses Small Batch Select Kentucky Straight Bourbon Whiskey 52% ABV (104 proof)

MASH BILL: OBSV

Four Roses Single Barrel 50% ABV (100 proof)

Above: Four Roses Small Batch Kentucky Straight Bourbon Whiskey.

IF YOU TRY ONE...

Four Roses Small Batch Kentucky Straight Bourbon Whiskey 45% ABV (90 Proof)

The nose has fruity notes with a hint of acetone, but underlying these initial aromas are notes of burnt oak and lots of vanilla. On the palate, it starts with a slightly astringent and green character, followed by some heat on the tongue. As the heat dissipates, sweetness ramps up leading to a big hit of spice. On the finish, it lingers for a long time, with notes of oak and vanilla. Overall, this is a nice bourbon that is well balanced, easy to drink and generally an affordable price.

Jim Beam American Stillhouse

Clermont, KY 37° 55' 52.8" N, 85° 39' 08.7" W

After Prohibition, James Beauregard Beam purchased the Murphy Barber Distillery in Clermont, and together with his son Jeremiah and his nephew Carl Beam, he rebuilt and refurbished the distillery in just 120 days. Production at the distillery began in the spring of 1935 with plans to sell the resurrected Old Tub brand and a new brand named Jim Beam. By 1946, Jeremiah was running the growing business, selling bourbon at home and overseas. Then in 1987, Beam purchased National Distillers, giving them ownership of the Old Crow and Old Grand-Dad Bourbon brands, as well as Old Grand-Dad's high-rye bourbon mash bill, which they still make today. Fast-forward to 2014, when Suntory Holdings purchased Jim Beam, forming Beam Suntory, one of the largest producers of distilled spirits in the world.

WHISKEYS

MASH BILL: 75% CORN, 13% RYE, 12% MALTED BARLEY

Jim Beam Kentucky Straight Bourbon Whiskey

– **Black Extra-Aged** 43% ABV (86 proof) Jim Beam Black Label dropped its 8-year-age statement in 2015.

– **Double Oak** 43% ABV (86 proof) Four-year-old bourbon is vatted and then refilled into 'freshly' charred barrels to continue its maturation.

– **Devil's Cut** 45% ABV (90 proof) Bourbon absorbed by the barrel is extracted and blended with their 'extra-age' bourbon for a more 'robust' flavour.

– **Bonded** 50% ABV (100 proof)

– **Single Barrel** 47.5% ABV (95 proof)

– **Repeal Batch** 43% ABV (86 proof)

Old Crow Kentucky Straight Bourbon Whiskey 40% ABV (80 proof)

Old Tub Bottled in Bond Kentucky Straight Bourbon Whiskey 50% ABV (100 proof)

Legent Kentucky Straight Bourbon Whiskey Partially Finished in Wine & Sherry Casks 47% ABV (94 proof)

SMALL BATCH COLLECTION:

Basil Hayden's Kentucky Straight Bourbon Whiskey
– **Artfully Aged** 40% ABV (80 proof)
– **Aged 10 Years** 40% ABV (80 proof)

Baker's Single Barrel Kentucky Straight Bourbon Whiskey
– **Aged 7 Years** 53.5% ABV (107 proof) Before 2019, Baker's had been vatted from multiple barrels. Now each barrel selected for the brand is proofed to 107 and bottled individually.
– **Limited Edition Aged 13 Years** 53.5% ABV (107 proof)

Booker's Kentucky Straight Bourbon Whiskey ABV and age vary
Since its first release, this had been a single-barrel cask-strength bourbon that included a barrel code, but in 2015

Below: Jim Beam American Stillhouse, Clermont, Kentucky.

Opposite above: Jim Beam Bourbon Bottling Plant, Clermont, Kentucky.

Opposite below: Workers load barrels of bourbon on to a truck at The Jim Beam Distillery.

Beam Suntory began naming and numbering their releases to capitalize on the bourbon collector craze.

Knob Creek Kentucky Straight Bourbon Whiskey
– **Aged 9 Years** 50% ABV (100 proof) Beam dropped its 9-year-age statement in 2016 due to a lack of sufficiently aged whiskey to meet demand, but the age statement was reintroduced at the beginning of 2020.
– **Aged 12 Years** 50% ABV (100 proof)
– **Single Barrel Reserve Aged 9 Years** 60% ABV (120 proof)

MASH BILL: 63% CORN, 27% RYE, 10% MALTED BARLEY

Old Grand-Dad Kentucky Straight Bourbon Whiskey
– **Original** 40% ABV (80 proof) In 2013, the ABV dropped from 43% (86 proof) to 40% ABV (80 proof).
– **Bonded** 50% ABV (100 proof)
– **114** 57% ABV (114 proof)

IF YOU TRY ONE...

Old Tub Bottled in Bond Kentucky Straight Bourbon Whiskey
50% ABV (100 proof)

Immediately on the nose there are notes of baked apples covered in a heavy dusting of cinnamon, mixed with a touch of vanilla and seasoned oak. On the palate, it is warm with notes of pastry, green apple skins and a hint of blackberry intermingled with a toasted oak flavour reminiscent of cut timber. The finish lingers with notes of baked apple and soft, warm baking spices and oak. A nice bourbon that is likely to please those who are looking for apple spice and oak flavours. The first impression is like drinking a warm apple strudel and it is good to see Old Tub move from a distillery exclusive into wider distribution for others to enjoy. This will work well in several classic cocktails such as a Manhattan or Old-Fashioned, and homemade eggnog if you are so inclined. In addition, the light fruity and woody notes would also be a pleasant addition to a spiked hot apple cider or hot toddy as the weather turns colder.

Above: Old Tub Bottled in Bond Kentucky Straight Bourbon Whiskey.

Kentucky Artisan Distillery

Crestwood, KY 38° 20' 11.5" N, 85° 27' 47.3" W

In 2012, Steve Thompson, Chris Miller and Mike Loring founded Kentucky Artisan Distillery (KDA) with the vision of creating Kentucky's first contract distillery for 'people to come and bottle their dreams'. Built inside the Crestwood, Kentucky Ice Cream Distributors, KAD was designed to produce as little as a single barrel or as much as 1,800 barrels a year depending on what their clients needed. One of their early clients was Castle Brands, the owner of Jefferson's Bourbon, and after a couple of years, Castle purchased a 20 per cent ownership stake in KAD, helping to guarantee its future supply for Jefferson. Then in 2019, Pernod Ricard acquired Castle Brands and their ownership stake in KAD.

WHISKEYS

MASH BILL: UNDISCLOSED

Jefferson's Very Small Batch Blend of Straight Bourbon Whiskeys 41.5% ABV (83 Proof)

Jefferson's Reserve Very Old Kentucky Straight Bourbon Whisky Very Small Batch 45.1% ABV (90.2 proof)

Jefferson's Ocean Aged at Sea Kentucky Straight Bourbon Whiskey Very Small Batch 45% ABV (90 Proof)

Iron Quarter Kentucky Straight Bourbon Whiskey 44% ABV (88 proof)

Above: Jefferson's Very Small Batch Blend of Straight Bourbon Whiskeys.

IF YOU TRY ONE...

Jefferson's Very Small Batch Blend of Straight Bourbon Whiskeys

41.5% ABV (83 Proof)

The aroma is bright and fruity with notes of baked apple, vanilla and a touch of oak. On the palate, the taste is light with a semi-sweet flavour of caramel that slowly fades with soft oak tannins. This is a somewhat simple, oak-forward bourbon that mellows nicely with a little water or in a cocktail.

Maker's Mark Distillery

Loretto, KY 37° 38' 49.7" N, 85° 21' 06.1" W

The Maker's Mark Distillery was founded by Bill and Margie Samuels in 1953. In 1975, Bill Samuels, Sr turned the reins of the company over to his son Bill, Jr, who is credited with transforming Maker's Mark into an internationally recognized brand. During the 1980s, Maker's Mark was sold a few times, while the family maintained control of production. In 2005, Maker's joined the Beam portfolio of bourbons. In 2010, after 57 years of producing only one bourbon, Maker's expanded their line adding Maker's 46, which takes the regular aged bourbon and finishes it in re-coopered barrels with added French oak staves (the individual pieces of wood that make up a barrel). The following year, Bill Samuels, Jr retired and his son Rob Samuels was promoted to the role of chief operating officer.

Above: Maker's Mark employees hand dip bottles of the bourbon with their signature red wax on the bottling line at the Maker's Mark Distillery plant in Loretto, Kentucky.

MASH BILL: 70% CORN, 16% RED WINTER WHEAT, 14% MALTED BARLEY

Maker's Mark Kentucky Straight Bourbon Whisky
- **Original** 45% ABV (90 proof)
- **Cask Strength** ABV varies
- **46** 47% ABV (94 proof)

IF YOU TRY ONE...

Maker's Mark Kentucky Straight Bourbon Whisky

45% ABV (90 Proof)

The aroma is light with sweet notes of syrup and light brown sugar, which open to notes of corn, oak and spiced honey. On the palate, it is refreshingly dry and woody, with a lasting warmth and notes of vanilla, butterscotch and toasted oak. The finish is warming and lingers with flavours of mild oak and spice. A classic bourbon profile with a sweet nose and oak-focused palate, though it is not astringent or bitter in any way. Enjoy with ice or in a classic cocktail.

Above: Maker's Mark Kentucky Straight Bourbon Whisky.

Wild Turkey Distillery

Lawrenceburg, KY 38° 02' 37.4" N, 84° 51' 10.8" W

According to legend, Thomas McCarthy, an executive at the Austin Nichols company, brought some barrel samples of bourbon with him on a wild turkey hunt. The sourced bourbon was so popular that they released it to the public in 1942 as a new brand. In 1971, Austin Nichols purchased the distillery that had been supplying bourbon for Wild Turkey, then in 1980 both companies were sold to Pernod Ricard of France. In 2009, Wild Turkey was purchased by Gruppo Campari of Italy, which invested $100 million in a new distillery, warehouses, bottling plant and visitor centre. For almost all of this time, one man has been involved in making Wild Turkey 101: Jimmy Russell, who started working at the then-named J.T.S. Brown Distillery, rising in the ranks to become Wild Turkey's master distiller in the late 1960s. While Jimmy has yet to retire, his son Eddie Russell was named master distiller in 2015. A year later, the actor Matthew McConaughey joined Wild Turkey as their creative director, and with the help of Jimmy and Eddie, they released Longbranch, which adds the step of filtering the bourbon with mesquite charcoal from the native Texan's home state.

WHISKEYS

MASH BILL: 75% CORN, 13% RYE, 12% MALTED BARLEY

Wild Turkey Kentucky Straight Bourbon Whiskey

– **81** 40.5% ABV (81 proof)

– **101** 50.5% ABV (101 proof)

– **Rare Breed Barrel Proof** ABV varies

– **Kentucky Spirit Single Barrel** 50.5% ABV (101 proof)

– **Master's Keep Bottled In Bond Aged 17 Years** 50% ABV (100 proof)

– **Master's Keep Revival Finished in Oloroso Sherry Casks** 50.5% ABV (101 proof)

Below: Wild Turkey Distilling Co. Lawrenceburg, Kentucky.

Russell's Reserve Kentucky Straight Bourbon Whiskey
- **10 Years Old** 45% ABV (90 proof)
- **Single Barrel** 55% ABV (110 proof)
- Vintage ABV vary

Longbranch Kentucky Straight Bourbon Whiskey 43% ABV
(86 proof) Filtered with oak and Texas mesquite charcoal.

IF YOU TRY ONE...

Longbranch Kentucky Straight Bourbon Whiskey
43% ABV (86 proof)

On the nose, there are notes of bright green apple, rich maraschino cherries, caramel, butterscotch, vanilla and warm toasted oak. On the palate, it is simultaneously sweet and woody with notes of fresh sweet corn, cinnamon and baked apple, with just a touch of vanilla. The finish has fruit notes of fresh peach, vanilla and a hint of smoky wood that ends with a slight acidity that makes your mouth water for more. Longbranch is a nice extension to the Wild Turkey line. And although the mesquite charcoal does not impart the same smoky flavour found in barbecue, there is a definite impact on the whiskey compared with the standard Wild Turkey 101. Overall, tasty and easy to drink neat, while working with ice or in any bourbon cocktail. For the price, it is also an accessible choice for those who enjoy a more fruit-forward bourbon with a good balance of wood and spice.

Above: Longbranch Kentucky Straight Bourbon Whiskey.

WESTERN KENTUCKY

Dueling Grounds Distillery

Franklin, KY 36° 42' 23.3" N, 86° 34' 20.7" W

Marc Dottore founded Dueling Grounds Distillery in 2013 after a successful career in the country music business. A few years earlier, Dottore had visited a few distilleries in Kentucky, and with his home brewing experience decided to open a distillery. After studying the craft and business side of the industry, he purchased a 25-US-gallon (95-litre) still and began making gin, liqueurs and white whiskey while his bourbon aged. Today, Dueling Ground uses a 200-US-gallon (757-litre) still and recently released their four-year-old Linkumpinch Kentucky Straight Bourbon. The name refers to a farm near the Kentucky–Tennessee border that was used as a duelling site in the 19th century to settle 'matters of honour', even though both states had laws against the practice.

WHISKEYS

MASH BILL: WHEATED BOURBON MASH

Linkumpinch Kentucky Straight Bourbon Whiskey 50% ABV (100 proof)

Linkumpinch Single Barrel Cask Strength Kentucky Straight Bourbon Whiskey Aged 4 Years ABV varies

IF YOU TRY ONE...

Linkumpinch Kentucky Straight Bourbon Whiskey
50% ABV (100 proof)

The aroma is a mixture of young corn, grass and dry oak, and underneath are notes of sweet cherry and vanilla. On the palate, the whiskey's youth is evident with notes of fresh corn husk and green oak, combined with sweet flavours of stone fruit, caramel, vanilla and clove. On the finish, there are flavours of pipe tobacco, vanilla and young oak tannins. Linkumpinch is showing some very nice fruit and barrel notes, though overall it is still a bit immature. As it continues to age, the young corn and oak flavours will no doubt develop and integrate better. If you like younger bourbons that are more on the green side, then this will scratch that itch. For now, it is probably best used in cocktails.

Above: Linkumpinch Kentucky Straight Bourbon Whiskey.

The Mint Julep evolved from a Persian beverage (*c.*AD 900) made with rosewater and sugar to refresh the drinker. As the drink moved west, other botanicals and alcohol were introduced until it reached Virginia where it took the form we know today of mint, bourbon, sugar and crushed ice. Kentucky has had a long love affair with the Mint Julep. Around 1847, Henry Clay, the US Senator from Kentucky, introduced the cocktail to the staff of the Willard Hotel in Washington DC to the delight of his colleagues in the Capitol, and in 1938, the Mint Julep became the official drink of the Kentucky Derby.

The Mint Julep

MAKES 1

7.5–30ml (¼ –1fl oz) **simple syrup**, depending on preferred level of sweetness

6–10 **mint leaves**, depending on size of leaves

60–90ml (2–3fl oz) **bourbon**

1 **mint sprig**, to garnish

Add the simple syrup and mint leaves to the bottom of a Julep cup or tall glass. Gently bruise the leaves with a muddler to release their oils, but not so much that they break into small pieces. Fill the cup or glass halfway with crushed ice. Add the bourbon and stir to combine the ingredients. Fill the rest of the cup or glass with crushed ice and stir until the outside appears frosted. Top up with more crushed ice, garnish with a mint sprig and add a short straw.

Tip: You can make crushed ice by using a Lewis bag or by wrapping ice cubes in a clean tea towel and crushing them with a rolling pin or mallet.

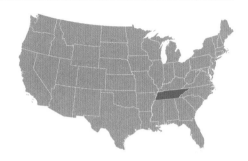

Tennessee
Whiskey

Since about 1982, one brand of Tennessee whiskey has maintained its position as the bestselling American whiskey both in the United States and worldwide. But despite the individual success of Jack Daniel's, Tennessee whiskey has largely been an unsung hero in the broader story of American whiskey. It is possible that only having two major producers of the style for most of the 20th century damaged the overall category. However, an infusion of new blood and the flowering of craft distilleries has helped to reignite interest in the broader category of Tennessee whiskey.

History

At the time of European exploration of what today is the United States, the region we know as Tennessee was occupied by several tribes including the Chickasaw, Choctaw and Cherokee. But despite their presence, the British and French both laid claims to the region and built competing forts and trading posts to establish control.

Opposite: A cabin in the Great Smoky Mountains National Park, Tennessee, during autumn.

Climatic conditions: Lynchburg, TN – home of the Jack Daniel's Distillery

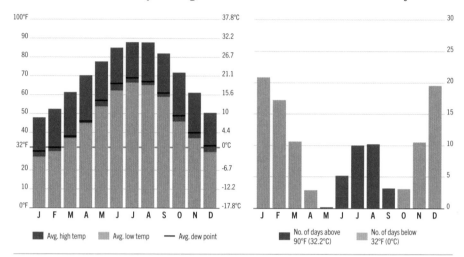

| ■ Avg. high temp | ▨ Avg. low temp | — Avg. dew point | ■ No. of days above 90°F (32.2°C) | ▨ No. of days below 32°F (0°C) |

This geopolitical conflict erupted into war that spread across five continents and ultimately laid the ground for the 13 American colonies declaring independence and forming the United States of America.

On 1 June 1796, Tennessee was admitted as the 16th state to the Union. Settlers continued to pour in looking for land, some of which was purchased from tribes, some negotiated in treaties and some taken by force. The state developed a mixed agricultural economy that included cotton and tobacco farming powered by slave labour, cattle and horse rearing and subsistence farming.

As was common practice in this era, Tennessee farmers distilled excess grain into whiskey that could

Region Name:	State of Tennessee
Nickname:	The Volunteer State
Capital City:	Nashville
Population:	6,829,174
Number of Active Distilleries:	55
Whiskey Fact:	In 2020, Tennessee had over 3 million barrels of ageing whiskey valued at more than $5 billion.

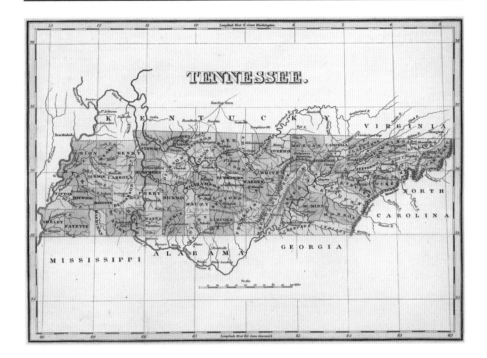

be bartered or sold for other goods and services. Corn (maize) cultivation, which had spread throughout the region between AD 900 and 1600, allowed the Indigenous Peoples in the area to transition to an agricultural system centred around permanent settlements and villages. So naturally, as American settlers cleared land for farming, they included corn in the mix of grains they grew. Corn was so well adapted to the region that by 1840, Tennessee had become the number one producer in the country. And with the growing supply of corn, more and more of it was transformed into whiskey and sold as a commercial product for cash.

Before the widespread use of charred oak barrels to purposely alter the flavour and colour of whiskey, early American distillers developed a few strategies to improve the final product. These early whiskeys were known for being a bit rough, and in response distillers used multiple distillations, sour mashing and filtering of the fresh spirit with charcoal – or even sand, gravel, paper or wool – to

Above: An official map of the state of Tennessee, drawn in 1827.

Right: A late 1880s photo showing Jack Daniel (centre with white hat) at his distillery in Tennessee. The man to his right is believed to be George Green, son of Nathan 'Nearest' Green, who taught Daniel how to make whiskey.

enhance its character. And eventually this practice found its way to Tennessee.

There seems to be good evidence that the technique of filtering whiskey using sugar maple charcoal was brought to south central Tennessee by William Pearson. Pearson claims he learned the practice from his mother, who in turn learned it from her mother, Mary Stout Jacocks of Pennsylvania. This is quite plausible, given that at the time it was common for women in the household to be brewers and distillers. In 1812, aged 51, Pearson moved from South Carolina where he had been living and settled near what today is Flat Creek, Tennessee in Bedford County. Pearson's family documents record that he sold his whiskey recipe and filtering technique to Alfred Eaton around 1825. Eaton was a distiller based in Lynchburg, not far from where Jack Daniel would eventually build his distillery.

Today there are competing claims about who taught Jack Daniel about filtering his whiskey through sugar maple charcoal. Some claim that he learned the technique directly from Eaton, while others say it came from 'Nearest' Green, the slave who taught Daniel how to make whiskey (see page 76). It seems unlikely we will ever know with certainty. Either way, this method of filtering new whiskey became so entrenched in the area that it was known as the Lincoln County Process, named after the county where Jack Daniel and other distillers made their whiskey.

However, at the same time that the whiskey business was growing in Tennessee, there was also a growing sentiment for temperance and outright prohibition. During the period after the American Civil War known as Reconstruction, Tennessee's governor, who was also a Methodist minister, preached the evils of liquor. Momentum for prohibition continued to build until 1909 when the state legislature enacted a law banning the manufacture of intoxicating beverages and the sale of liquor within 4 miles (6.4km) of schools, churches and hospitals, eventually closing more than 300 distilleries a full 10 years before the ratification of the 18th Amendment.

After the end of National Prohibition, Tennessee continued to enforce state laws that limited the production and sale of alcohol and did not lift the statewide ban on the manufacture of alcohol until 1937. Even then, the law did not clear the way for distillers to restart production, but a minimum of ten per cent of qualified voters were required to petition the county court to hold a referendum, and a majority of qualified voters in the county had to vote for allowing the manufacture of liquor. Once that hurdle

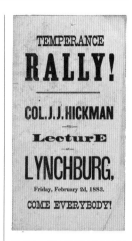

Above: A temperance rally poster, Lynchburg, Tennessee.

JACK DANIEL'S OLD NO. 7

When Jack Daniel and Dan Call registered their distillery with the federal government, they were listed as the seventh distillery in Tennessee's fourth tax district. Then as today, barrels of whiskey were labelled with their distillery number, No. 7 in Daniel's case, which identified where the whiskey came from once it was sold. However, the government later decided to combine districts four and five, the latter covering the area around Nashville, which at the time had several large distilleries. Because of this reorganization, Daniel's distillery number was changed to 16. Not wanting to lose his loyal customers, he began labelling his barrels and bottles with 'Old No. 7' to remind them that even though his distillery number had changed, it was still the same whiskey.

was cleared, the distiller would have to pay a $1,000 fee to the state, the county and, if the distiller was located inside city boundaries, the municipality as well. $3,000 during the Great Depression was no small sum, equalling about $54,000 (£40,000) in 2020. With all these barriers to entry, it is not surprising that only the Motlow family who owned Jack Daniel's had the means to restart production in 1938, followed 21 years later by Cascade Hollow (see page 74) in 1959.

For almost all the remaining 20th century, Jack Daniel's and George Dickel, made at Cascade Hollow, were the only Tennessee whiskeys produced in the state. But in 1997, Phil Prichard opened a distillery in Kelso (see page 81), and began making his version of Tennessee whiskey. Only recently has Tennessee begun to loosen its rules around distilling, passing a law in 2009 that increased the number of counties allowing the manufacture of liquor from 3 to 44 of the state's 95 counties.

Following the law's passage, the number of distilleries in the state has grown significantly and yet less than a

Below: Bottles of George Dickel whiskey are displayed on a shelf at a beverage outlet.

dozen of them sell a spirit labelled as Tennessee whiskey. Given the formidable size and funding of both Jack Daniel's and George Dickel, one can imagine it would take a person of incredible confidence to place a bottle of their Tennessee whiskey next to those celebrated brands and believe the drinking public will pick up theirs. But that is beginning to happen with a few small distilleries. In addition, some new life has been breathed into older brands, first with the resurrection of Nelson's Green Brier Distillery (see page 80). A once prominent brand, Green Brier did not survive state prohibition, though almost exactly a hundred years later the company was restarted by descendants of the original owner. Then in 2017, Fawn Weaver helped to keep the rediscovered legacy of Nearest Green alive by launching an award-winning Tennessee whiskey in his honour, followed by the construction of a new distillery bearing his name (see page 78). More recently in 2018, Diageo appointed Nicole Austin to be the general manager and distiller at Cascade Hollow Distillery. A trained chemical engineer, and former head blender for Kings County Distillery, Austin has helped drive renewed interested in George Dickel with the releases of extra-aged bottled-in-bond expressions of the Tennessee whiskey. And as more new whiskeys come to market, from every corner of the state, they will further demonstrate that Tennessee whiskey is not just another bourbon made outside Kentucky but its own distinct regional style of American whiskey.

Production requirements

If you look at the Federal Standards of Identity for Distilled Spirits, you will find detailed production requirements for bourbon, rye whiskey, malt whiskey, blended whiskey and even less well-known types such as light whiskey and spirit whiskey. However, you will not find a definition for Tennessee whiskey. The first legal definition of Tennessee Whiskey was in the North American Free Trade Agreement (NAFTA) between the US, Canada and Mexico. NAFTA, which was agreed upon in 1992 and became law in 1994, defined Tennessee whiskey as a straight bourbon whiskey unique to the State of Tennessee. This definition can be found in all other subsequent trade agreements with the United States that include provisions on distilled spirits. But then on 13 May 2013, the State of Tennessee passed a law elaborating on the required production processes for a spirit to be labelled as Tennessee whiskey. The new law includes the same federal standards as for bourbon: minimum 51% corn mash, distilled at not more than 160 proof (80% ABV), stored in new charred oak barrels at not more than 125 proof (62.5% ABV) and bottled at no less than 80 proof (40% ABV). In addition, the law stipulates that the whiskey must be manufactured in Tennessee, and that the new make spirit must be filtered through sugar maple charcoal prior to ageing. This latter requirement, colloquially known as the Lincoln County Process, has for the past two hundred years been the defining feature that distinguished bourbon from Tennessee whiskey. Interestingly, Prichard's Distillery received an exemption because their Tennessee whiskey has never been filtered using maple charcoal before ageing (see page 82).

EAST TENNESSEE

Knox Whiskey Works

Knoxville, TN 35° 58' 02.8" N, 83° 55' 22.7" W

Founded in 2015, Knox Whiskey Works is dedicated to working with local farmers and artisans to produce unique spirits that represent Knoxville and East Tennessee. They source hickory cane and Tennessee Red Cob corn, which is grown in Jefferson County along the Holston River and then stone ground by a local mill. In addition to their Tennessee Whiskey, Knox Whiskey Works also produces bourbon, corn whiskey, gin and a few liqueurs and flavoured whiskeys.

WHISKEYS

MASH BILL: 100% LOCALLY GROWN HEIRLOOM CORN

Gold Release Tennessee Whiskey 50% ABV (100 proof)

IF YOU TRY ONE...

Gold Release Tennessee Whiskey 50% ABV (100 proof)

On the nose the whiskey is rich and spicy, with aromas of corn bread covered in warm butter and cinnamon followed by just a touch of vanilla and caramel. On the palate, the whiskey has lots of flavour – spicy and sweet barrel notes intermixed with corn bread, and fruit notes from the grain. The whiskey is lush and rich with just the right amount of heat, and a hint of chocolate malt on the finish. Overall, this is an excellent whiskey that is big, bold and packs in lots of flavour. The Hickory Cane corn makes a delicious whiskey and, even though it is bottled at 45%, fans of barrel-strength whiskey will really enjoy this.

Above: Gold Release Tennessee Whiskey.

Cascade Hollow Distilling Company

Tullahoma, TN 35° 26' 18.5" N, 86° 14' 46.0" W

The Cascade Hollow Distillery was founded by John F Brown and F E Cunningham in 1877 just outside Tullahoma, and they began production the following year. One of their wholesale clients was the Nashville-based Geo. A. Dickel & Co., run by a German-born immigrant and his brother-in-law Victor Emmanuel Shwab. In 1888, Shwab purchased an ownership share in the distillery, making Geo. A. Dickel & Co. the distributor of their popular Cascade Whisky. However, in 1910, Tennessee enacted statewide prohibition of alcohol, so Shwab moved production of Cascade Whisky to the Stitzel Distillery in Louisville, until Kentucky enacted its own prohibition in 1917. After the repeal of National

Below: The welcome centre at the Cascade Hollow Distilling Company, the home of George Dickel Tennessee Whisky.

Prohibition, Shwab sold the Cascade Whisky brand to the Schenley Distillers Corporation who built a new Cascade Hollow distillery about a mile (1.6km) from the original site in Tullahoma. Whiskey production began on 4 July 1959, and the first bottle of George Dickel Tennessee Whisky was released in 1964. Subsequently, ownership changed hands a couple of times before, in 1997, Diageo acquired the distillery and the George Dickel brand.

WHISKEYS

MASH BILL: 84% CORN, 8% RYE, 8% MALTED BARLEY

George Dickel Superior No. 12 Sour Mash Tennessee Whisky
45% ABV (90 proof)

George Dickel Classic No. 8 Sour Mash Tennessee Whisky
40% ABV (80 proof)

George Dickel Barrel Select Tennessee Whisky 43% ABV (86 proof)

George Dickel Bottled in Bond Tennessee Whisky 50% ABV
(100 proof)

IF YOU TRY ONE...

George Dickel Bottled in Bond Tennessee Whisky 50% ABV (100 Proof)

The nose is rich and dense with notes of rum raisin, dried orange peel, burnt sugar and *vin santo*. At first sip, the whiskey explodes on the palate with baking spice flavours and coats the mouth with soft and sweet notes of vanilla and toffee. On the finish, it ends with warm flavours of clove and roasted nuts. There is also a very faint acidity that leaves you wanting to take another sip just as the flavour of the whiskey fades away. After ageing for 11 years, George Dickel's Fall 2008 Bottled in Bond Tennessee Whisky is a powerhouse of flavour. At 50% ABV, it is not hot and even with its extra age it is not over-oaked. Instead, it seems to have picked up the best aspects of the barrel, pulling spice and depth without that raw woodiness sometimes found in older American whiskeys.

Above: George Dickel Bottled in Bond Tennessee Whisky

Jack Daniel's Distillery

Lynchburg, TN 35° 17' 03.6" N, 86° 22' 00.5" W

Jasper Newton 'Jack' Daniel was born around 1850, close to Lynchburg. When Daniel was a young boy, he went to work for a local Lutheran preacher named Dan Call who owned a farm and a distillery in the area. Daniel was put to work in the distillery and Call instructed his head distiller, a hired slave named Nathan 'Nearest' Green, to teach Daniel the trade. In 1875, Daniel and Call rebuilt the distillery and hired the now freed Green to work as their master distiller. In 1907, Daniel gave the distillery to Lemuel Motlow and another of his nephews, who ran the company until 1910 when state prohibition forced them to close. By 1938, Motlow had become a Tennessee state senator and worked to repeal prohibition and restart the distillery. However, the distillery was only in operation for a couple of years before they ceased production, this time because of World War II. Finally, in 1956, the Motlow family sold Jack Daniel's to Brown-Forman, which controls it to this day.

Below: A charcoal wood fire at the Jack Daniel's Distillery, Lynchburg, Tennessee.

WHISKEYS

MASH BILL: 80% CORN, 8% RYE, 12% MALTED BARLEY

Jack Daniel's Old No. 7 Tennessee Whiskey 40% ABV (80 proof)
Bottling strength has gradually changed over time, from
90 proof before 1987, 86 proof from 1987–2002 and 80 proof
from 2002 to the present, presumably to allow more whiskey
to be bottled.

Jack Daniel's Gentleman Jack Tennessee Whiskey 40% ABV
(80 proof)

Jack Daniel's Bottled-in-Bond Tennessee Whiskey 50% ABV
(100 proof) Only available through travel retail.

Jack Daniel's Single Barrel Tennessee Whiskey
– **Select** 47% ABV (94 proof)
– **100 Proof** 50% ABV (100 proof)
– **Barrel Proof** ABV varies May be higher ABV depending on
the release.

Jack Daniel's Sinatra Select Tennessee Whiskey 45% ABV (90 proof)

*Above: The visitor centre at
the Jack Daniel's Distillery,
Lynchburg, Tennessee.*

Jack Daniel's Bottled-in-Bond Tennessee Whiskey

50% ABV (100 proof)

Intense fruity aromas of raspberries, dried peaches and bright red cocktail cherries, verging on Bazooka bubblegum, with a light note of toasted wood. On the palate, it has nice notes of sweet fresh fruit, barrel spice, vanilla and light tannins to balance the sweetness. It lingers on the tongue with notes of sweet cinnamon, nutmeg, bright red cherries and warm oak flavours. For older fans of Jack Daniel's who miss the higher bottling strength, this bottled-in-bond expression is a glimpse of its former glory and why Jack became the bestselling American whiskey in the world. While it is currently restricted to travel retail sites for those flying internationally, it is one of the best expressions of Jack Daniel's currently available, and hopefully Brown-Forman will extend its distribution for more to enjoy.

Above: Jack Daniel's Bottled-in-Bond Tennessee Whiskey.

Nearest Green Distillery

Shelbyville, TN 35° 34' 36.4" N, 86° 26' 42.9" W

In 2018, construction began on the Nearest Green Distillery at the Sand Creek Farm in Shelbyville. The distillery is part of a long-term project to honour and revive the legacy of Nathan 'Nearest' Green, the former slave who taught Jack Daniel how to make whiskey and served as Daniel's first master distiller. While Green's story was not exactly hidden, his influence on Jack was not widely spoken of either. Then in 2016, a story in the *New York Times* caught the eye of Fawn Weaver, an author and real estate investor. Within a year, Weaver established a foundation in Green's name, and launched Uncle Nearest 1856 Premium Whiskey. While the initial whiskey was sourced and blended from a couple of Tennessee distilleries, Weaver built a team to develop the brand and the distillery, and oversee the production of their own whiskey even before the distillery was finished. On 14 September 2019, phase one of the distillery opened to the public. Today, the 1856 expression is a blend of Tennessee whiskeys aged between 8 and 14 years that go through a unique double-filtration process before bottling. In addition to 1856, Nearest Green offers an unaged version of their future whiskey, an 1820 Single Barrel whiskey and an 1884 Small Batch whiskey that is blended by Victoria Eady Butler, a fifth-generation descendant of Nearest Green and now master blender for the company.

WHISKEYS

MASH BILL: RYE BOURBON MASH

Uncle Nearest 1856 Premium Whiskey Silver 45% ABV (90 proof)
Aged one day.

Uncle Nearest 1856 Premium Whiskey 50% ABV (100 proof)

Uncle Nearest 1820 Premium Whiskey Aged 11 Years Single Barrel ABV varies

Uncle Nearest 1884 Small Batch Whiskey 46.5% ABV (93 proof)

IF YOU TRY ONE...

Uncle Nearest 1856 Premium Whiskey
50% ABV (100 proof)

The nose has a very nice, sweet aroma of caramel, corn bread and charred oak. At 50% ABV, you notice the alcohol, but it does not overpower the aromas. As the whiskey breathes, you get a lovely floral perfumed aroma of white peaches and a mix of roses and irises. As it crosses your tongue, there is a pleasant, sweet flavour of fruit mixed with nutmeg, followed by a hint of chocolate caramel. These flavours are supported by a solid oak character, which has a very slight greenness to it that overall provides an earthy balance. It ends in a light fruity character of raspberries and candy floss, with an underlying mellow woodiness. This is a very enjoyable whiskey that does a good job of honouring the memory of its namesake. Not only is it soft enough to sip neat, but the flavour is also robust enough to carry through an Old-Fashioned, a Manhattan or any other classic whiskey cocktail.

Above: Uncle Nearest 1856 Premium Whiskey.

Nelson's Green Brier Distillery

Nashville, TN 36° 09' 49.3" N, 86° 47' 53.8" W

In 2006, Andy and Charlie Nelson went with their father Bill to a butcher in Greenbrier, Tennessee. Across from the butcher was an old warehouse and a historical marker telling the story of how Charles Nelson, Andy and Charlie's great-great-great-grandfather, built a distillery there and made some of the most popular Tennessee whiskey in the state. Their passion was ignited and in 2009 they reopened Nelson's Green Brier Distillery. During the time they have been distilling and ageing their wheated Tennessee whiskey, they have been selling Belle Meade Bourbons, a line of sourced whiskey that they finished in a variety of wine and spirit casks. In 2017, they released Nelson's First 108 Tennessee Whiskey, commemorating the 108-year closure period. Two years later, they released their flagship brand Nelson's Green Brier Tennessee Whiskey, with a near-identical label to the one their ancestor used back in the 1860s, completing their more than decade-long journey. That same year, Constellation Brands purchased a majority stake in the distillery, while Andy and Charlie continue to run the day-to-day operations.

Above: Nelson's Green Brier Tennessee Whiskey.

WHISKEYS

MASH BILL: WHEATED BOURBON MASH

Nelson's First 108 Single Barrel Tennessee Whiskey ABV varies

Nelson's First 108 Tennessee Whiskey 45.2% ABV (90.4 proof)

Nelson's Green Brier Tennessee Whiskey 45.5% ABV (91 proof)

IF YOU TRY ONE...

Nelson's Green Brier Tennessee Whiskey
45.5% ABV (91 proof)

On the nose, it has an interesting savoury quality reminiscent of a corn salad with herbs and sweet heirloom tomatoes. As the whiskey breathes, more traditional aromas of caramel, oak, leather and corn bread rise from the glass. It has a great flavour of cinnamon, and tea sweetened with honey and a touch of caramel.

At 45.5% ABV, the whiskey is a touch hot on the finish, but there are lots of pleasant lingering flavours of vanilla, caramel, tobacco and oak. Nelson's Green Brier is a great return of a legendary whiskey. Charlie and Andy have done their ancestor justice and created a Tennessee whiskey that is a joy to sip on the rocks or use in any of your favourite cocktails.

Prichard's Distillery

Kelso, TN 35° 07' 39.1" N, 86° 27' 42.9" W

In 1993, Phil Prichard began exploring the idea of opening a distillery, in part due to his family's distilling heritage reaching back to Benjamin Prichard who willed his stills to his son Enoch in 1822. By 1997, Phil Prichard had received all his appropriate licences and opened his distillery in Kelso, making it the first new distillery in the state in almost four decades. From the beginning, Prichard has made a variety of spirits including rum, liqueurs, flavoured whiskey and of course Tennessee whiskey. Prichard saved his first barrels of Tennessee whiskey to age and be released on his tenth anniversary, making it only the third brand of Tennessee whiskey produced in the state since Prohibition. Prichard's whiskey is different in that it is primarily made from white corn, and it goes into the barrel without first being filtered through sugar maple charcoal. Since the passage of the 2013 state law defining Tennessee whiskey, his is the only whiskey allowed to use the moniker without requiring the Lincoln County Process (see page 72). Those early barrels of ten-year-old whiskey have long since sold and today Prichard's Tennessee whiskey is vatted from a mix of barrels no less than three years old.

WHISKEYS

MASH BILL: RYE BOURBON MASH WITH WHITE CORN
Benjamin Prichard's Tennessee Whiskey 40% ABV (80 proof)

IF YOU TRY ONE...
Benjamin Prichard's Tennessee Whiskey
40% ABV (80 proof)

At first sniff, it is super fruity with aromas of glacé cherries, strawberries, bubblegum, candy floss (cotton candy) and lavender, while underneath all of that fruitiness is a faint hint of oak. On the palate, the fruity character carries over with a hint of blueberry moderated by the barrel, with added baking spice flavours. The finish is soft with a lingering flavour of Bubblicious Watermelon Gum, oak and bright cinnamon. It seems that Prichard's use of white corn has really amped up the fruity esters. At around three years old, this is a solid choice for fans of Jack Daniel's or those who like very fruity bourbons.

Above: Benjamin Prichard's Tennessee Whiskey.

Tenn South Distillery

Lynnville, TN 35° 21' 01.6" N, 87° 01' 02.5" W

In 2009, the Tennessee state legislature passed a law that opened up the opportunity for distilleries to be licensed in the 41 wet counties that allowed the sale of alcohol

but had not gone the extra step to permit the production
of distilled spirits. Inspired by the new law, two friends,
Clayton Cutler and Blair Butler, an engineer and a
radiologist by trade, began exploring the idea of opening
their own distillery. During the process, they purchased
a 28-acre (11.3-hectare) plot in Lynnville and a pot still,
and embarked on the licensing process while they
studied their new craft. They officially opened in 2013
and immediately started laying down barrels of future
Tennessee whiskey, selling vodka and moonshine to pay
the bills. Like all other Tennessee whiskey distillers, they
filter their new make through a container of sugar maple
charcoal before it goes into the barrel. Tenn South uses a
fairly large size of charcoal, as they claim that it helps to
add a smoky quality to the whiskey rather than mellowing
it before entering the barrel. They then fill their new make
whiskey into a combination of 15-, 25- and 53-US-gallon
(57-, 95- and 200-litre) barrels, blending them together to
get the right flavour for each bottling.

WHISKEYS

MASH BILL: WHEATED BOURBON MASH WITH WHITE CORN

Clayton James Tennessee Whiskey 45% ABV (90 proof)

IF YOU TRY ONE...

Clayton James Tennessee Whiskey
45% ABV (90 proof)

At first, the nose is somewhat closed with a subtle
aroma reminiscent of cooked masa from tamales and a
green note like steamed chayote squash. As the whiskey
breathes, the greenness dissipates and more notes of
hickory, tobacco and black pepper come to the fore.
Overall, it is youthful with lots of grain flavours, notes
of oak and a touch of sweet tea. The finish has a definite
smoke note like burnt oak or hickory that lingers on the
tongue, along with the flavour of boiled sweet young corn.
Clayton James is a nice whiskey that is showing a bit of its
youth still, though that will probably fade over time. Drink
on the rocks or mix into a cocktail like the Lynchburg
Lemonade (see overleaf).

Above: Clayton James Tennessee Whiskey.

Created in 1980 by Tony Mason at Tony Mason's Restaurant & Lounge in Huntsville, Alabama, this drink pays homage to Lynchburg, Tennessee, the home town of the Jack Daniel's Distillery. It became the subject of two lawsuits, in 1983 and 1987, between Mason and Brown-Forman, the owner of Jack Daniel's, but in the end a jury found that Mason could not claim the recipe as a trade secret.

Lynchburg Lemonade

MAKES 1

45ml (1½fl oz) **Tennessee whiskey**

30ml (1fl oz) **triple sec**

30ml (1fl oz) **lemon juice**

lemon-lime soda, to top up

lemon wedge or **wheel**, to garnish

Fill a tall glass such as a highball or Collins glass with ice, then pour over the whiskey, triple sec and lemon juice. Top up the glass with a lemon-lime soda and give a quick stir to mix the ingredients. Garnish with a lemon wedge or wheel.

Texas
Bourbon

The story of Texas is a massively important touchstone in the culture of the United States. One significant part of that story includes the dusty cantinas and Western saloons where heroes and villains often meet to fight for control. In these depictions, you sometimes see men standing at the bar pouring shots from blank bottles, presumably of tequila or whiskey. These brandless bottles are fitting considering that, while it is certain there were distilleries making whiskey in the state, there are no well-known brands or whiskey men whose stories survived Prohibition till today. In some ways, this lack of tradition has served as a *tabula rasa* for the 21st-century distillers on which to create and experiment while the public gets to taste the imprint of Texas on the bourbons that she makes.

Opposite: Since the 19th century, windmills have been used throughout Texas and the Great Plains to pump water to the surface from subterranean aquifers for cattle and crops.

Depending on the location, Texas can experience some extreme temperature fluctuations, which have a significant impact on the character of whiskeys aged there. It is not unheard of for the temperature in a single

Climatic conditions: Blanco County, TX – 6 active distilleries

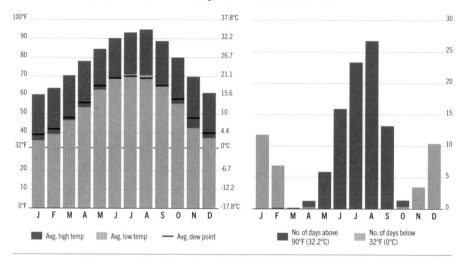

Avg. high temp   Avg. low temp   — Avg. dew point

No. of days above 90°F (32.2°C)   No. of days below 32°F (0°C)

day to start below freezing and by the afternoon reach upwards of 80°F (27°C). Texas can also experience very dry periods followed by hurricanes that release a deluge of rain. These extremes result in an increased interaction between the spirit and the barrel that speeds up certain aspects of maturation. Because of the Texas climate, just copying Kentucky or Tennessee distilling and ageing practices would not make sense. So, today's best Texas bourbons are distilled and aged with their specific climate in mind, producing bold and expressive whiskeys that honour the character and legacy of their state.

History

When Spanish explorers arrived in what would become Texas, they encountered several tribes that cultivated corn (maize). Indigenous to southern Mexico, corn has been cultivated as a food crop for about 10,000 years and spread into South America and north to the east coast of the United States. The Indigenous Peoples located along what is now the Gulf Coast of Texas were a crucial link in the gradual migration of corn cultivation from the south into the northeast of the continent. However, by the time American settlers began arriving in Texas, they

Region Name:	State of Texas
Nickname:	The Lone Star State
Capital City:	Austin
Population:	28,995,881
Number of Active Distilleries:	163
Whiskey Fact:	Ageing barrels of Texas whiskey have been known to lose all their contents due to evaporation (angel's share) in as little as seven years.

had already developed their own cultivation practices and know-how to ferment and distil the grain into the whiskey.

By the time of Texas statehood in 1845, subsistence and commercial farmers were growing millions of bushels of corn per year, most of which was concentrated in the eastern part of the state. As the population grew, so did cultivation of other grains, and in 1859, the corn harvest

Below: An official map of the state of Texas, drawn in 1912.

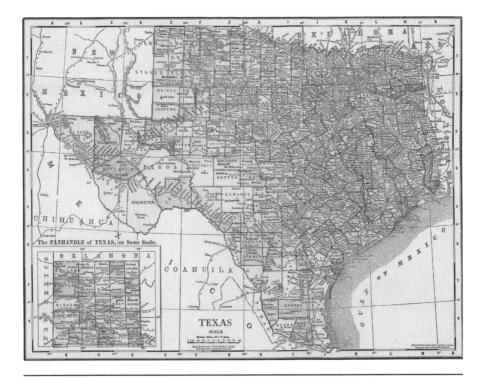

Above: American saloon keeper and justice of the peace, Phantly Roy Bean, Jr, at his courthouse saloon along the Rio Grande River in a desolate stretch of the Chihuahuan Desert of West Texas around 1870.

was only six times greater than all other grains grown in the state, as opposed to the 25-times margin it enjoyed a decade earlier. Newspaper reports and adverts from this period show whiskey distilleries spread across the state, but they do not share any specifics about how it was made.

Even before statehood, the Temperance Movement had a strong presence in Texas and succeeded in growing support county by county. Between 1843 and 1911, various Temperance organizations such as The United Friends of Temperance, Woman's Christian Temperance Union and Anti-Saloon League failed to enact statewide prohibition, but succeeded in growing the total number of dry counties in the state. By 1910, 214 of the state's counties had enacted some form of total or partial prohibition, leaving only 25 wet counties. In 1913, Texas elected Morris Sheppard, a strong advocate of prohibition, to the US Senate, and three years later, Texas sent a few new congressmen to the House of Representatives who supported a constitutional amendment. This growing political support for National Prohibition culminated in a dry victory when Texas ratified the 18th Amendment on 4 March 1918 and then passed their own statewide prohibition on 24 May 1919, though by that time all legal distilleries in the state had already closed.

After Prohibition ended, Texas-based alcohol production resumed in three phases. Almost immediately after Repeal, breweries reopened and began making and selling their ales and lagers. Then in the 1970s, several wineries were established, looking to make fine wines from locally grown grapes, but there were no whiskey distilleries. Finally, in the early 2000s, Dan Garrison began exploring the idea of making bourbon in Texas. He spent a few years learning the process and getting all the appropriate licences before distilling his first batch of a wheated bourbon mash in 2007. A year later, Chip Tate founded Balcones Distilling and in 2009 released Baby Blue Corn Whiskey, making it the first legally made Texas whiskey sold in the state since before Prohibition (see page 93). Since then, the number of Texas distillers making whiskey and bourbon has continued to grow, offering devotees of the spirit new expressions to explore.

Above: Balcones Baby Blue Corn Texan Whiskey.

Production requirements

According to a plain reading of the federal labelling requirements for distilled spirits, a Texas bourbon would simply be a bourbon whiskey produced in conformity with the Standards of Identity in the State of Texas. However, several blenders and rectifiers have been able to capitalize on the mystique of Texas. One can find bottles draped in imagery and words associated with the Lone Star State, while the liquid inside actually comes from Kentucky, Tennessee or Indiana. For a few inscrutable reasons, the same regulations that strictly define bourbon do not always require the exact origin of the spirit to be stated on the label. Because of this, a group of Texas distillers formed an organization called the Texas Whiskey Association (TXWA), which has created a trademark for Certified Texas Whiskey™. The intent is that those who are making real Texas whiskey can proudly display the certification on their label and separate out their products from the other whiskeys that claim Texas provenance but are not actually distilled and aged in the state. However, because this is a certification controlled by a private organization, and not a state law, there are some real Texas whiskeys that for a variety of

Above: Corn and other grains are milled into a fine powder before they are cooked at Treaty Oak Distilling, Dripping Springs, Texas.

personal, political, production or business reasons have not applied for the certification.

For a spirit to claim that it is a Certified Texas Whiskey™, it must meet all the following criteria. First, the whiskey must be produced at a licensed distillery in Texas. The whiskey must be made from a mash of cereal grains and Texas-sourced water that is completely fermented, distilled, barrelled and matured in Texas, in compliance with the Federal Standards of Identity. After maturation, the whiskey must be bottled in Texas with 'no additives other than Texas-sourced water'. And lastly, an administrative employee of the TXWA must verify that this process was followed before the whiskey is certified.

Distilling and maturing whiskey in Texas offers some interesting challenges and benefits, so to know who has done it and done it well is valuable information. Relying on a voluntary certification will probably never fully capture every real Texas whiskey. However, for those interested in exploring how the varied agricultural, geographic and climatic conditions of a big state like Texas impact on the flavour of its bourbon, it is an excellent place to start.

NORTH TEXAS

Balcones Distilling

Waco, TX 31° 33' 01.6" N, 97° 08' 08.3" W

Chip Tate founded Balcones Distilling in 2008 inside an old welding shop, building most of the equipment himself. Tate's first spirit was Baby Blue Corn Whiskey distilled from 100% roasted Hopi blue corn and aged for 6 months in a small barrel. Even though he opened three years after Dan Garrison's Garrison Brothers Distillery (see page 91), the short ageing time allowed him to get Baby Blue into the market earlier, making it the first Texas distilled whiskey since before Prohibition. After a very public battle with his board of directors, Tate left Balcones in 2014 and has moved on to new ventures. Since then, Jared Himstedt, who has been at Balcones from the beginning, has taken over as head distiller and blender. Balcones is now in a new

Below: Balcones Distilling, Waco, Texas.

location and they have expanded their whiskey portfolio to include bourbon, rye and single malt whiskeys as well as several more annual releases. Balcones has received several awards, including being named Craft Distillery of the Year three times by *Whiskey Magazine*.

WHISKEYS

MASH BILL: 100% HOPI BLUE CORN

Balcones Texas Blue Corn Straight Bourbon Whiskey ABV varies

MASH BILL: HOPI BLUE CORN, TEXAS RED WINTER WHEAT, TEXAS RYE, MALTED BARLEY

Balcones Texas Pot Still Straight Bourbon Whiskey 46% ABV (92 proof)

MASH BILL: HOPI BLUE CORN, TEXAS RED WINTER WHEAT, GOLDEN PROMISE MALTED BARLEY

Balcones Texas Wheated Pot Distilled Straight Bourbon Whiskey ABV varies

Above: Balcones Texas Pot Still Straight Bourbon Whiskey.

IF YOU TRY ONE...

Balcones Texas Pot Still Straight Bourbon Whiskey

46% ABV (92 proof)

The nose is rich with strong, sweet aromas of caramel, butter toffee and caramel popcorn, while underneath are earthy notes of oak and dry hay. On the palate, the flavour quickly jumps between blue corn tortillas, caramel, dried corn husk, vanilla, burnt oak and baking spices. The finish is warm and sweet, with lingering notes of butterscotch and honeyed apple. This is a big and sumptuous whiskey that shows flashes of youth, which are quickly overwhelmed by the sweet corn and candied notes.

Firestone & Robertson Distilling Co.

Fort Worth, TX 32° 42' 07.4" N, 97° 17' 11.6" W

Founded in 2010 by Leonard Firestone and Troy Robertson, Firestone & Robertson Distilling Co. makes unique Texas bourbon. They quickly brought in Rob Arnold to serve as their head distiller, who at the time was working towards a Ph.D in biochemistry. With Arnold's expertise, they were able to domesticate a wild yeast

strain found on a pecan nut that could fully ferment their wheated bourbon mash and produce a flavour profile they really enjoyed. Initially their whiskey was distilled to barrel proof in a single pass using a hybrid pot–column still. Their TX Texas Straight Bourbon was first released in January 2017 just as it passed the 4-years-old mark and bottled at 45% ABV (90 proof). That same year, they completed construction of their new Whiskey Ranch built on the 112-acre (45-hectare) Glen Garden Country Club. With room to expand, they installed a 50-ft (15-m) column still and converted one of their old hybrid stills into a doubler, which will allow them to produce 40 barrels a day compared with 3 barrels at their original distillery. In 2019, Firestone & Robertson was purchased by Pernod Ricard.

Above: Employees package TX Texas Whiskey at the Firestone & Robertson whiskey ranch in Fort Worth, Texas.

WHISKEYS

MASH BILL: WHEATED BOURBON MASH

TX Texas Straight Bourbon Whiskey

– **Original** 45% ABV (90 proof)

– **Barrel Proof** ABV varies

– **Finished in PX Sherry Casks** 50.8% ABV (101.6 proof)

– **Finished in Tawny Port Casks** 50.8% ABV (101.6 proof)

TX Texas Straight Bourbon Whiskey
45% ABV (90 proof)

The nose is very fragrant with notes of vanilla and dried fruit, followed by aromas of baked bread and fresh apple with an underlying oak character that adds structure. The palate starts sweet with notes of caramel and apple, which is well balanced by flavours of oak and pepper spice. The finish is warm, semi-sweet and long with notes of oak and spice, with a hint of dark plum. Overall, this is a spicy, semi-sweet bourbon with a healthy dose of oak, probably most appealing to those who like theirs oak-forward with a touch of sweetness. Drink neat or use in your favourite cocktail.

Above: TX Texas Straight Bourbon Whiskey.

HILL COUNTRY

Milam & Greene Whiskey

Blanco, TX 30° 06' 45.4" N, 98° 25' 05.5" W

Marsha Milam launched Ben Milam Whiskey in 2017, named after the Kentucky native who became a hero of the Texas Revolution, and the following year founded Milam & Greene with head blender Heather Greene, master distiller Marlene Holmes and head brewer Jordan Osborne. The business quickly evolved to include distilling their own Texas bourbon from a unique mash bill of 70% Texas corn, 22% Pacific Northwest malted rye from Oregon and Washington and 8% Wyoming malted barley, and aged in charred new oak barrels for a minimum of two years. Just seven barrels were tapped in August 2020 to make the inaugural release of their cask-strength bourbon, though hopefully there are many more where those came from.

WHISKEYS
MASH BILL: 70% CORN, 22% MALTED RYE, 8% MALTED BARLEY

Milam & Greene Distillery Edition Straight Bourbon Whiskey
60.9% ABV (121.8 proof)

Milam & Greene Distillery Edition
Straight Bourbon Whiskey 60.9% ABV (121.8 proof)

Featuring a deep, wonderful aroma of butterscotch and caramel, with just a hint of alcohol, which is not too surprising at over 60% ABV, this whiskey also has a pleasant whiff of lightly toasted English muffin. On the palate, it is supple with only a little heat, speaking to the great attention with which it was distilled. There are flavours of vanilla, cinnamon and caramel, combined with notes of cherry and fresh peach, like a gourmet version of candy corn but more refined. After the sweeter flavours, a good dose of seasoned oak comes in to balance the profile. It lingers with a long finish of cinnamon and nutmeg sprinkled over honeyed corn bread, and a splash of fresh orange juice. Bold and powerful while still retaining elegance and balance, this bourbon sets a new high water

Below: Milam & Greene Distillery Edition Straight Bourbon Whiskey.

mark in Texas whiskey. It would be a shame to mix this precious nectar, so please savour it neat, or with a dash of water if the alcohol feels too intense. Ice might close the bourbon and hide some of its excellence. If you have the opportunity to buy a bottle, do yourself a favour and do not pass it up.

Treaty Oak Distilling

Dripping Springs, TX 30° 14' 48.4" N, 98° 03' 16.7" W

Daniel Barnes founded Treaty Oak Distilling in 2006, inspired by the work ethic of his parents and driven by his own entrepreneurial spirit. The distillery takes its name from the five-hundred-year-old oak tree where it is told that Stephen F Austin signed a treaty with local tribes of Indigenous Peoples to define the boundaries of American settlement in Texas. Treaty Oak began by distilling and selling their rum, vodka and Waterloo Gin, and then in

Below: Treaty Oak Distilling, Dripping Springs, Texas.

2016, they moved to the 28-acre (11.3-hectare) Ghost Hill Ranch just north of Austin and built a larger distillery with room to age whiskey. Two years later, Treaty Oak released their first batch of Ghost Hill Bourbon, named after the ranch, as well as sourcing whiskeys from other distillers in the United States and in Canada. That same year, Treaty Oak partnered with the Mahalo Spirits Group to update its packaging and expand its distribution, and in 2019, the distillery released a 40% ABV expression of their bourbon that they call The Day Drinker.

WHISKEYS

MASH BILL: 57% TEXAS YELLOW DENT CORN, 32% TEXAS WHEAT, 11% MALTED BARLEY

Treaty Oak The Day Drinker Texas Bourbon Whiskey 40% ABV
(80 proof)

Treaty Oak Ghost Hill Texas Bourbon Whiskey 47.5% (95 proof)

IF YOU TRY ONE...

Treaty Oak Ghost Hill Texas Bourbon Whiskey
47.5% (95 proof)

The aroma is slightly closed with light notes of caramel, vanilla and cherries. As the whiskey opens, there are more aromas of oak and malt whiskey. On the tongue, it is sumptuous with a full body and dripping with caramel, and as it moves across the palate, there are more pronounced oak tannins with light flurries of cinnamon, clove and vanilla. As it lingers, there is a subtle mixture of stone fruits like peach and cherry followed by a warm flavour of toasted oak, dark chocolate and hazelnuts (think Nutella but with less sugar), and just a hint of bright mint. At only 18 months, Ghost Hill is an impressive whiskey full of great flavours and good integration that should improve with slightly longer ageing, though they would also run the risk of extracting too much oak flavour from the barrel in the Texas heat. This is both the skill and the conundrum of Texas bourbon – it can be excellent at a year and a half, but the greater potential that comes with longer maturations could also spell disaster. At 47.5% ABV, this is easy to enjoy neat and would be excellent for Old-Fashioneds, Manhattans or even an Improved Whiskey Cocktail.

Above: Treaty Oak Ghost Hill Texas Bourbon Whiskey.

Gulf Coast Distillers

Houston, TX 29° 45' 41.6" N, 95° 18' 39.0" W

Originally founded in the 1920s as a coffee company, the business was expanded into distilling by the de Aldecoa family in 2014 with the creation of Gulf Coast Distillers. Carlos de Aldecoa hired consultant and master distiller Dave Pickerell to help them develop their mash bills and distillation protocols. Gulf Coast produces several vodkas, gin and whiskey brands including Giant whiskeys. Giant Texas Bourbon is distilled from a high-rye bourbon mash bill. And because of their proximity to the Gulf of Mexico, their whiskeys age in a hot and tropical climate with a high angel's share, so they do not take as long to mature as those in colder climates.

WHISKEYS

MASH BILL: 75% CORN, 21% RYE, 4% MALTED BARLEY

Giant Texas Bourbon Whiskey
– **Black Label** 40% ABV (80 proof)
– **Special Reserve Gold Label** 45.5% ABV (91 proof)
– **95 Pot Still** 47.5 (95 proof)

Billy Banks Single Barrel Cask Strength Bourbon Whiskey
56.5% ABV (113 proof)

Roughneck Small Batch Bourbon Whiskey 40% ABV (80 proof)

MASH BILL: 100% CORN

Hickory Hill Single Barrel Cask Strength Bourbon Whiskey
ABV varies

Above: Giant 95 Pot Still Texas Bourbon Whiskey.

IF YOU TRY ONE...

Giant 95 Pot Still Texas Bourbon Whiskey 47.5% (95 proof)

The nose is similar to a lightly aged corn whiskey with an earthy aroma of corn mush combined with light aromas of unripe peach, oak and fresh mint. On the palate, it has a more traditional bourbon profile with flavours of creamed corn, caramel, cinnamon and clove. It starts sweet on the tongue, and as it moves back there is a pronounced hit of oak tannins mid-palate that helps balance the initial sweetness. The finish is light with lasting flavours of nectarine, oak and a hint of mint at the very back of the palate. For those looking for a spice-forward bourbon with a good balance of youthful fruit character and oak, this will do the job. Enjoy on the rocks or with your favourite mixer.

Yellow Rose Distilling

Pinehurst, TX 29° 47' 18.4" N, 95° 27' 22.8" W

Ryan Baird, Troy Smith and Randy Whitaker founded Yellow Rose Distilling just outside Houston in 2010 and launched their first whiskeys two years later. Their Outlaw Bourbon is unique in that it is distilled from a mash of 100% Texas-grown corn, which is then aged for six months in 10-US-gallon (38-litre) barrels before being vatted and bottled at 46% ABV (92 proof). Between the small barrels and the intense Texas climate, Outlaw bourbon extracts a lot of colour and flavour in a very short period.

WHISKEYS

MASH BILL: 100% CORN

Yellow Rose Outlaw Bourbon Whiskey 46% ABV (92 proof)

Yellow Rose Premium Collection Bourbon Whiskey 43% ABV (86 proof)
– #1 Port Barrel Finish
– #2 Cabernet Sauvignon Finish

IF YOU TRY ONE...

Yellow Rose Outlaw Bourbon Whiskey 46% ABV (92 proof)

The nose is very fruity with apple and a hint of bubblegum. The palate starts sweet with notes of vanilla and apple and then begins to dry out with a big wallop of spice. The finish is long and semi-sweet, with flavours of oak and baking spice. This is a surprisingly good bourbon for its youth. It also demonstrates the complexity that can come from a 100% corn whiskey, pot distilled and aged in intense conditions. Those that like spicy or oak-forward bourbons can enjoy it neat, but it will also work in several cocktails.

Above: Yellow Rose Outlaw Bourbon Whiskey.

In the 19th century, several travellers observed Texans drinking in a wide array of grog shops, taverns, saloons and ornate hotel lounges. Texan grog shops were most likely simple drinking establishments that served beer and a few simple cocktails, 'grog' being a term used to describe a mixture of spirits, water and citrus juice. Given that grapefruit, oranges and a variety of other citrus fruits have grown in the Rio Grande Valley on Texas's southern border since the time of Spanish colonization, and early Texans were known for their fondness for whiskey, it is not a stretch to imagine locals mixing these simple ingredients to make a refreshing drink.

Texas Grog

MAKES 1

60ml (2fl oz) **bourbon**

60ml (2fl oz) **cold water**

15ml (½fl oz) **freshly squeezed orange juice**

15ml (½fl oz) **simple syrup**

2 dashes **Angostura bitters**

Put all the ingredients into a cocktail shaker, fill with ice and shake. Strain into a double Old-Fashioned glass filled with ice.

Missouri
Bourbon

While the legal definition of Missouri bourbon was created as recently as 2019, the Show-Me State has a long and colourful relationship with whiskey, though that story has often been overshadowed by its neighbours to the east. The varied geography of the state provides vast areas of fertile farmland well suited for growing corn (maize), while the southern Ozark Mountains provide much of the American white oak used to make premium whiskey barrels. Today's Missouri distillers are tapping into the state's natural and cultural history to write a new chapter in the story of Missouri whiskey and demonstrate the particular character it has to offer.

History

In May 1804, Lieutenant William Clark, co-leader of the Corps of Discovery, made note of the arrival of a keel boat from Kentucky carrying barrels of whiskey and other supplies. The notation comes just as he, Captain Meriwether Lewis and the rest of their party were

Opposite: Downtown skyline, Kansas City, Missouri.

Climatic conditions: St Louis, MO – 7 active distilleries

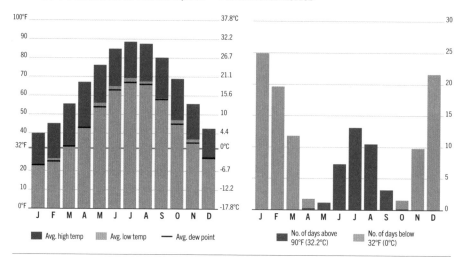

Avg. high temp   Avg. low temp   — Avg. dew point

No. of days above 90°F (32.2°C)   No. of days below 32°F (0°C)

beginning their expedition up the Missouri River to traverse the newly acquired Louisiana Territory, and chart a route to the Pacific Ocean. While Clark does not specify the type of whiskey on the keel boat, one can assume that it was some type of corn whiskey or proto-bourbon, given its origin in the Bluegrass State.

For the next two hundred years, the story of whiskey in Missouri was largely to be dominated by rectifiers and bottlers of imported bourbon and rye, with a couple of notable exceptions. One of the most famous 19th-century Missouri whiskey bottlers was David Nicholson, a Scottish immigrant who found his way to St Louis and in 1843

Region Name:	State of Missouri
Nickname:	The Show-Me State
Capital City:	Jefferson City
Population:	6,137,428
Number of Active Distilleries:	48
Whiskey Fact:	The state's 2019 Missouri bourbon law makes it only the third state to enact legislation specifying how its name can be used in relation to whiskey.

Above: An official map of the state of Missouri, date unknown.

co-founded a grocery business that also sold wine and liquor. Nicholson built a reputation for his good taste, blending and bottling Kentucky bourbon under his 1843 brand. An advertisement from that time shows that at least some of his whiskey was sourced from W.A. Gaines & Co. in Frankfort, Kentucky, the distiller for Old Crow bourbon. Nicholson proved to be so successful that his 1843 whiskey was even being sold in the Waldorf Astoria Hotel in New York City.

Interestingly, several of Missouri's most prominent pre-Prohibition whisky rectifiers and bottlers were immigrants who settled in the Show-Me State. George Stark, born in Germany's Rhine-Hesse wine region, emigrated to the US and settled in Hermann, about 80 miles (129km) west of St Louis. After successfully guiding the Stone Hill Winery to becoming the third largest wine producer in the world, Stark and his sons purchased an ownership stake in the Tom Moore distillery located in Bardstown, Kentucky. They shipped the whiskey to their St Louis warehouse and rebottled

THE WHISKEY RING

In October 1869, President Ulysses S Grant appointed former General John McDonald as the St Louis area supervisor of the US Treasury Department's Internal Revenue Service and to help increase support for the president. Shortly after his arrival, General McDonald realized that if he under-reported the amount of whiskey sold, he could keep the excise tax on the difference. His scheme did not go unnoticed and within a year or so it had involved hundreds of people at all levels of the government and liquor industry, including distillers, distributors, liquor merchants, gaugers, revenue agents and clerks in the Treasury Department. As more men were brought into the Whiskey Ring, it diluted the shared profit and required more tax money to be diverted. They accomplished this by bringing distillers and revenue men from as far away as New Orleans, Chicago, Peoria, Milwaukee and Cincinnati into their network, siphoning off $1–2 million a year. Ultimately, the scheme was discovered, resulting in 110 convictions and the recovery of more than $3 million.

it under several brands including their flagship brand Old Stark Whiskey. Similarly, another German immigrant, named Jacob Barzen, settled in Kansas City, and in 1884 opened a liquor retail and wholesale business with his partner Isaac Glasner. Glasner & Barzen built an expansive mail order business that sold Kentucky bourbon and Pennsylvania rye bottled under dozens of brands in Alaska, Colorado, Iowa, Nebraska, New Mexico, Texas, Wisconsin and Wyoming. The business grew so rapidly that in 1903, Glasner & Barzen purchased the Blue Valley Distillery Co. in Leeds, Missouri and began selling bottled-in-bond expressions of Blue Spring Rye and Blue Springs Bourbon. By 1908, Glasner & Barzen had annual revenues of nearly $1 million (roughly $28 million/£20.4 million today), making them one of the most successful liquor companies in the state.

A Kentucky native named George Shawhan moved his family to Lone Jack, Missouri (east of Kansas City) in 1872 and built a two-barrel-a-day distillery. His business grew, but in 1900 Shawhan's distillery burned down, though luckily his warehouse with 800 barrels of whiskey survived. With his inventory intact, he was able to purchase the Holladay Distillery in Weston, Missouri (northeast of Kansas City), which had been built by Benjamin Holladay, the transportation magnate. With the Holladay Distillery, Shawhan expanded his portfolio to include ten brands of corn whiskey, rye and an old-style sour mash bourbon he claimed dated back to 1786. Eight years after purchasing the distillery, Shawhan sold it to the Singer family who ran the business until Prohibition. After Prohibition, the Singers reopened the distillery and in 1942 changed the name to the McCormick Distilling Company, under which it has remained in operation to this day, though the ownership has changed hands a few more times.

Between the end of National Prohibition and the beginning of the 21st century, McCormick was one of the only distilleries operating in the state, but over time their business model shifted away from distilling to importing, blending and bottling spirits. In the early 2000s, as with every other state in the Union, the craft distilling movement had reached Missouri and a few new distilleries began popping up looking to offer new and local expressions of Missouri whiskey. One of the first was Spirits of St. Louis founded by Steve Neukomm in 2007. Neukomm already had a successful brewpub, and when he expanded into making whiskey, American single malt

Right: Stacks of white oak (Quercus alba) logs at a stave mill in Missouri.

whiskey was an obvious choice, since he already had much of the equipment needed. Not long after this, a number of other distillers like Ralph Haynes and Tom Anderson of Pinckney Bend Distilling and Gary Hinegardner of Wood Hat Spirits (see page 114) looked to Missouri-grown varieties of heirloom corn to give their whiskeys unique flavours. And as the number of Missouri distillers continued to grow, the next natural question was what unique signature does the state leave on the whiskey made here? The answer came, at least partially, with the passage of a new state law defining Missouri bourbon whiskey.

Production requirements

On 11 July 2019, Governor Mike Parson signed House Bill 266, creating the first state specification of production requirements for whiskey to be labelled Missouri bourbon. The law stipulates that in addition to meeting the Federal Standards of Identity for bourbon, the whiskey must be mashed, fermented, distilled, aged and bottled in Missouri; aged in oak barrels manufactured in the state; and 100% of the corn used in the mash must be grown in Missouri.

The idea that inspired the bill came much earlier. Gary Hinegardner of Wood Hat Spirits had worked as an agronomist for a farmers' co-op, helping them grow corn to be sold around the country and internationally. He then

Above: Combine harvesting corn in Marshall, Missouri.

Left: Corn unloaded from a truck into the grain elevator at the Mid-Missouri Energy ethanol plant in Malta Bend, Missouri.

spent 17 years managing a stave yard, where American white oak was split and cut into staves for barrels. From these experiences, Hinegardner realized that Missouri farmers were growing corn, some of which wound up making whiskey in Kentucky that was aged in barrels made from Missouri-grown oak, and then that bourbon was sold back to Missourians. Being in a state that could grow both the corn and the wood needed to make great bourbon inspired Hinegardner and other distillers to start their (ad)ventures. This level of synergy is not completely possible in other states and has the added benefit of supporting agricultural, logging, manufacturing, wholesale, retail and tourism jobs all within Missouri.

ST LOUIS

StilL 630 Distillery

St Louis, MO 38° 36' 60.0" N, 90° 11' 34.1" W

David Weglarz founded StilL 630 in 2012 as an outlet for his passion, intensity and creativity. Currently located in a former Hardee's restaurant and surrounded by a tasting bar, his self-built stills and barrels full of ageing spirits, Weglarz has garnered great critical success, with several of his spirits winning high honours in competitions. In 2020, his American Navy Strength Gin was named Best American Gin, and in 2017, his Monon Bell Bourbon Whiskey was named Best Bourbon at the American Distilling Institute's Judging of Craft Spirits. Always striving for excellence, Weglarz has dozens of experimental barrels of whiskey, rum, gin, brandy and agave spirits pushing the status quo and finding interesting and innovative combinations in the process.

WHISKEYS

MASH BILL: RYE BOURBON MASH

StilL 630 Missouri Straight Bourbon Whiskey Single Barrel
45% ABV (90 Proof)

MASH BILL: 70% CORN, 20% RYE, 10% MALTED BARLEY

StilL 630 Monon Bell Straight Bourbon Whiskey 45% ABV (90 Proof)

IF YOU TRY ONE...

StilL 630 Missouri Straight Bourbon Whiskey Single Barrel 45% ABV (90 proof)

With a lovely aroma of baked apple with cinnamon and other fruit, on the palate, it slides lightly over the tongue bringing flavours of caramel, oak and cooked porridge with stewed apples and spices. It lingers on the finish with notes of bright apple skins, unfiltered apple juice and cinnamon, with just a touch of honey. It tastes like

Above: StilL 630 Missouri Straight Bourbon Whiskey Single Barrel.

an explosion of autumn colours and crisp morning air captured in an amber liquid. Silky and full of flavour, it is the balance between notes of sweet fruit and wood spice that makes this bourbon a joy to drink. Enjoy neat, on the rocks or in any number of classic cocktails.

CENTRAL MISSOURI

Blacksmith Distillery

Lohman, MO 38° 31' 29.1" N, 92° 24' 18.9" W

Michael J Broker, Jr founded Blacksmith Distillery to carry on the legacy of his father, who among other things was a blacksmith, distiller and farmer. Broker and his team are dedicated to making a mixture of traditional whiskeys as well as contemporary vodka and gin. While they are serious about producing quality spirits, one look at their marketing tells you they also have a good sense of humour about their business. In 2020, they released Cole County 200 in celebration of the bicentennial of their home county.

WHISKEYS

MASH BILL: RYE BOURBON MASH

Blacksmith Distillery Black Anvil Bourbon Whiskey 45% ABV (90 Proof)

Blacksmith Distillery Cole County 200 Missouri Bourbon Whiskey 40% ABV (80 Proof)

Blacksmith Distillery Missouri 2021 Missouri Bourbon Whiskey 40% ABV (80 Proof)

IF YOU TRY ONE...

Blacksmith Distillery Black Anvil Bourbon Whiskey
45% ABV (90 proof)

Above: Blacksmith Distillery Black Anvil Bourbon Whiskey.

A bright and lively bourbon with a mixture of fruity and earthy aromas, there are notes of fresh plum and green grapes combined with those of vanilla, creamed corn, caramel and just a touch of cinnamon. It starts with a pronounced sweetness that transitions to bright fresh fruit and then to slightly deeper flavours of vanilla and cinnamon, though they remain relatively light. The finish fills the mouth with a warm spice sensation that fades into sweet fruit notes of raisin and nectarine and ends with a slight tartness that calls you back for another drink. This is a young and vibrant whiskey with lots of pleasant flavours. At 45% ABV, it can definitely be enjoyed neat, though a splash of water or a single ice cube might soften a little of the alcohol sting and enhance some of the underlying flavour. For those who like more fruit-forward bourbons, this is definitely one to look out for.

Wood Hat Spirits

New Florence, MO 38° 53' 52.5" N, 91° 26' 53.5" W

Founding Wood Hat Spirits in 2013, Gary and Katy Hinegardner have since built a true craft distillery, putting flavour over economics. They are committed to using local ingredients not for the cachet or because it is popular but because they deeply believe that Missouri-grown corn and oak have something unique to offer whiskey drinkers. Wood Hat treats corn like winemakers treat their grapes, planting a variety of heirloom corn varieties for what each can bring to the spirit in terms of its flavour and body. In 2018, Wood Hat Spirits Bloody Butcher Red Corn Whiskey was named Best American Whiskey at the American Distilling Institute's Judging of Craft Spirits.

WHISKEYS

MASH BILL: WHEATED BOURBON MASH

Wood Hat Spirits Bourbon Rubenesque Bourbon Whiskey
50% ABV (100 Proof) Made with blue corn.

Wood Hat Spirits Brew Barrel Bourbon Whiskey 45% ABV (90 Proof)

Wood Hat Spirits Twin Timbers Bourbon Whiskey Finished in Pecan Barrels 45% ABV (90 Proof)

Wood Hat Spirits Montgomery County Bourbon Whiskey
50% ABV (100 Proof) Made with yellow corn.

Wood Hat Spirits Bloody Dapper Missouri Bourbon Whiskey
50% ABV (100 Proof) Made with Bloody Butcher red corn.

IF YOU TRY ONE...
Wood Hat Spirits Bloody Dapper Missouri Bourbon Whiskey 50% ABV (100 proof)

The aroma is rich with notes of stewed stone fruit, prunes and raisins mixed with cinnamon, clove and a touch of vanilla, finished off with a light touch of oak. On the palate, it is very complex with notes of dried peaches, caramel and oak that dance around on your tongue. Afterwards, the finish is long and light considering its 50% ABV bottling strength. Initially there are some resinous, almost pine notes that soften it into a light woody character mixed with caramel, almost like licking residual vanilla ice cream from a ice lolly. At first glance, this may come across as a bit unrefined, but as it breathes and with a touch of water, it opens and shows a really complex character from both the mash and the barrel to create a unique expression of Missouri bourbon.

Above: Wood Hat Spirits Bloody Dapper Missouri Bourbon Whiskey.

George A Williamson created the Rickey at Shoomaker's in Washington, DC in 1883 for 'Colonel' Joseph K Rickey, who was a frequent drinker and eventual owner of the bar. Many of the details about Joe Rickey's life are unclear or contradictory. We do know that, after the Civil War, he started a family and put his love of gambling, drinking and smoking to good use by becoming a Democratic lobbyist. In interviews, Rickey claimed both that he preferred lime juice in his drink because it helped cool the blood, and that he only drank Rickeys with lemon juice because it helped tone the stomach. Whichever is true, Rickey made it clear that Gin Rickeys were a perversion since gin was 'a liquor no gentleman could ever bring himself to drink'.

Bourbon Rickey

MAKES 1

½ **lime**

45ml (1½fl oz) **bourbon**

soda water, to top up

Fill a highball glass with ice. Squeeze the juice from half a lime over the ice and drop the lime into the glass. Add the bourbon, top up with soda water, and give the drink a quick stir to mix the ingredients.

Indiana
Rye whiskey

Indiana rye whiskey is not a historically significant regional style of American whiskey on a par with Kentucky bourbon or Monongahela rye. But at the beginning of the 21st century, a series of unrelated business decisions surrounding Indiana distilled rye whiskey helped to catapult the entire category back into the consciousness of the American whiskey drinker. Over the last decade, sales of rye whiskey have grown by 1,275 per cent and Indiana rye has played a significant role in its meteoric rise. And while most of that whiskey has come from just one large distillery, craft distillers throughout the state are contributing to the evolving understanding of Indiana rye whiskey.

History

After the end of the American Civil War in 1865, Indiana developed into a major centre for manufacturing all sorts of goods including whiskey. Indiana's relatively flat terrain allowed for the construction of canals and railways to

Opposite: A covered bridge, Indiana.

Climatic conditions: Lawrenceburg, IN – 2 active distilleries

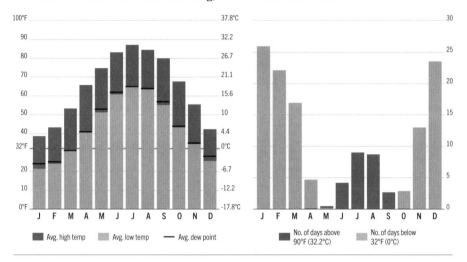

Avg. high temp   Avg. low temp   Avg. dew point   No. of days above 90°F (32.2°C)   No. of days below 32°F (0°C)

criss-cross the state, taking goods east and west, while the Wabash and Ohio Rivers enabled goods to move south down the Mississippi to New Orleans. Before Prohibition, Indiana had a large and prosperous distilling industry that produced large volumes of blended whiskey, rye and bourbon, and smaller quantities of fruit brandy and gin.

Not surprisingly, the largest Indiana distilleries were located on railway lines and near sources of water. Terra Haute was one such place. Located on the west side of the state, Terra Haute had a railway line that connected it to Indianapolis, and it sat along the east bank of the Wabash River, which flows south into the Ohio River. John H Beggs, who owned a successful distillery in

Region Name:	State of Indiana
Nickname:	The Hoosier State
Capital City:	Indianapolis
Population:	6,732,219
Number of Active Distilleries:	37
Whiskey Fact:	From 1935 to 2018 it was illegal to sell whiskey or any other alcohol on Sundays in the state.

Shelbyville, Indiana, moved to Terra Haute in the mid-1880s to purchase a controlling interest in the Wabash Distilling Company. Beggs's success caught the eye of the Whiskey Trust (see page 19) centred in Peoria, Illinois, where he eventually moved, becoming vice president of the Distilling and Cattle Feeding Company. But back in Indiana, some of Beggs's sons were busy running their own distilling and liquor businesses, one of which sold spirits treated with radium (see box, page 122)!

On the east side of the state in Lawrenceburg, a couple of distilleries were also steadily working away. One of these was the Rossville Distillery, founded in 1847. By 1906, the

Above: Botanical illustration of rye.

Rossville Distillery sold Rossville B Bourbon, Rossville B Rye, Rossville Rye Malt Whiskey and gin. But despite its success, Rossville closed in 1917, shortly before Indiana state prohibition took effect. For the next 15 years it sat dormant until a fire broke out and destroyed most of the plant.

Then in 1933, the Rossville site was purchased by Joseph E Seagram & Sons as part of the Canadian company's expansion into the United States. Seagram, like other Canadian distillers, was known for distilling and ageing several different whiskey mash bills separately. These spirits were known as flavouring whiskeys, which they would mix with neutral grain spirits to create their blended whiskeys. And because these flavouring whiskeys were made to be blended, they had to have strong flavours, which is why some of them had mash bills like 99% corn bourbon or 95% rye whiskey. These whiskeys were never meant to be bottled on their own but used like seasoning in a specific dish.

Introduced shortly after the end of Prohibition, Seagram's Seven Crown Blended Whiskey quickly became their bestseller, the first American whiskey to sell a million cases in a single year, and in 1983 they celebrated the sale of their three-hundred-millionth case. But business soured and in 2000, the 143-year-old company was forced to sell everything, with Pernod Ricard acquiring the Lawrenceburg distillery.

Once this distillery was divorced from the old Seagram liquor brands, its primary business became selling bulk spirits to other distillers and liquor brands such as

Templeton Rye in Iowa and High West Distillery in Utah. But things moved into high gear in 2011 with the release of Bulleit Rye Whiskey. The Bulleit brand had been a part of Seagram's portfolio since 1997 and ended up with Diageo in 2000. For most of that time, they only sold bourbon that came from the Four Roses Distillery in Lawrenceburg, KY (see page 49). Around the early 2000s, senior whiskey master Steve Beal saw the success Templeton and other brands were having and suggested to his bosses at Diageo that they add a 95% rye whiskey to the Bulleit line.

Bulleit Rye launched in 2011, and it was quickly followed by dozens of other brands bottling the same 95% rye mash bill. For decades, the only rye available was the 51% rye whiskeys made in Kentucky. The flavour profile of these new 95% ryes was more assertive and had lots of spice, which bartenders around the country loved using in classic drinks like the Sazerac, Vieux Carré, Old Pal and Boulevardier, and whiskey drinkers really enjoyed it. So, having the world's largest liquor company selling an excellent whiskey with a nice bottle and a good story has helped to make Bulleit the bestselling rye whiskey in the United States (see page 126).

Above: Seagram's Seven Crown American Blended Whiskey.

Below: MGP Distillery of Lawrenceburg, Indiana.

At the same time as the Lawrenceburg distillery was
changing hands, several craft distilleries began to pop
up around the state, initially selling unaged spirits like
vodka, gin and unaged fruit brandies while their whiskeys
aged. Like the pre-Prohibition distillers before them, this
new batch of craft distillers make a variety of whiskeys
including bourbon, corn whiskey, American single malt
and of course rye. It is still too early to say if Indiana rye
will become a lasting regional style of American whiskey,
but in the meantime there are plenty of good ones to taste.

Production requirements

The State of Indiana calls for no special production
requirements to label a spirit as Indiana rye whiskey. To
do so, the spirit must simply meet the Federal Standards
of Identity for rye whiskey and be produced in Indiana.
And according to US law, rye whiskey is defined as a
whiskey distilled no higher than 160 proof (80% ABV),
from a fermented mash of at least 51% rye grain, stored in
charred new oak barrels at no more than 125 proof (62.5%
ABV) and bottled no lower than 80 proof (40% ABV). In a
separate section of the regulations, they further stipulate
that any spirit labelled as straight rye whiskey must be
stored for a minimum of two years in a charred new oak

barrel and may not have any added harmless colouring/ flavouring/blending materials (HCFBM). Additionally, any bottled-in-bond (BIB) rye whiskey must comply with the added requirements that the whiskey in the bottle has to come from a single distillery, produced in one distilling season (spring is January–June, and fall is July– December), aged for at least four years in charred new oak barrels and reduced in strength only with the addition of pure water to 100 proof (50% ABV).

However, in yet another section of the regulations, it says that rye whiskey may contain HCFBM without being labelled. The regulation further stipulates that any HCFBM used must not exceed $2\frac{1}{2}\%$ by volume of the finished product. For rye whiskey (again this does not apply to straight rye or BIB rye), this means if a distiller chose to, they could use a small amount of caramel colouring and natural flavours to enhance the spirit. The Alcohol and Tobacco Tax and Trade Bureau (TTB) has explained that the use of HCFBM in rye whiskey is allowable because, while it is not an essential component of the spirit, it has been established through trade practice that a small volume of HCFBM is customarily used. Bourbon does not have this tradition, so no bourbon, straight bourbon or BIB bourbon may include any HCFBM. As an example, Templeton Rye (see page 130) has been transparent for some time in their marketing materials that they do include a small amount of HCFBM in their spirit, but they do not specify what they use, as is their right under the law.

NOT ALL SOURCED WHISKEY IS THE SAME

For more than a decade, MGP has been selling bulk whiskey to various companies. And while many of them are sourcing whiskey distilled from the same 95% rye mash bill, it is important to remember that every barrel in MGP's warehouses ages differently, let alone those that are shipped out of Indiana to continue aging or are subsequently finished in secondary barrels. The brands included on pages 126–33 that have sourced MGP rye illustrate how different aging environments, finishing barrels, blending choices and proofing can create very different flavour profiles that will appeal to different drinkers.

SOUTHERN LOWLANDS

Bulleit Distilling Company,
Shelbyville, KY

Lawrenceburg, IN 39° 05' 52.3" N, 84° 51' 38.3" W

The Bulleit brand was created by Tom Bulleit, a lawyer from Frankfort, Kentucky, who has claimed that his bourbon is based on a generations-old family recipe, though there is no independent historical evidence to support this. He sold the brand in 1997 to Seagram, which was later acquired by Diageo in 2001. In 2011, Diageo added its now famous 95 Rye Whiskey to the Bulleit portfolio. The rye whiskey is distilled by MGP

Below: Neon sign for Bulleit Frontier Whiskey in the Grand Central Market in downtown Los Angeles, California.

distillery in Lawrenceburg from a mash of 95% rye and 5% malted barley, which was originally meant as a flavouring whiskey for one or more of the old Seagram's blended whiskeys (see page 122). The rye used a green label, which has some historical basis, but since 2011 many new ryes that come to market use some sort of green on their label.

WHISKEYS

MASH BILL: 95% RYE, 5% MALTED BARLEY

Bulleit 95 Straight American Rye Whiskey 45% ABV (90 proof)

IF YOU TRY ONE...

Bulleit 95 Straight American Rye Whiskey
45% ABV (90 proof)

On the nose, there are notes of sweet cherries combined with aromas of oak and some muted spice character. At first sip, there is an initial fruit sweetness that quickly gives way to bolder wood flavours of oak and cloves. On the finish, there is a lingering flavour of oak and faint tannins, with just a hint of fresh peach. At 45% ABV, Bulleit Rye is warm and inviting without any sharpness from the alcohol. While the whiskey is more wood-forward than other ryes, it is not overpowering and opens well with a splash of water or on a large ice cube. Its bold and slightly fruity character make it a great choice for cocktails as well. While not the most outstanding rye, its quality, balance, versatility and affordability has understandably made it the bestselling rye whiskey in the United States.

Above: Bulleit 95 Straight American Rye Whiskey.

Cadée Distillery, Clinton, WA

Lawrenceburg, IN 39° 05' 52.3" N, 84° 51' 38.3" W

Colin Campbell, a Scotsman transplanted to the Pacific Northwest, founded Cadée Distillery on Whidbey Island in Puget Sound, less than 40 miles (64km) from Seattle. Campbell sources his whiskeys from other distilleries and allows them to mature in the maritime air of Puget Sound before vatting and bottling them. For his rye whiskeys, Campbell gets his whiskey supplies from the MGP distillery in Lawrenceburg, distilled from their 51% rye, 45% corn and 4% malted barley mash bill.

WHISKEYS

MASH BILL: 51% RYE, 45% CORN, 4% MALTED BARLEY

Cadée Straight Rye Whiskey 42% ABV (84 proof)

Cadée Cascadia Rye Whiskey Finished in Port Barrels 43.5% (87 proof)

Cadée Invictus Barrel Strength Rye Whiskey Finished in Oloroso Sherry Barrels 55% ABV (110 proof)

IF YOU TRY ONE...

Cadée Cascadia Rye Whiskey Finished in Port Barrels 43.5% (87 proof)

On the nose, there are floral, tea and fruit aromas like a combination of iced black tea with a touch of ripe plum and cherry blossoms, overlaid with a light toasted oak note. On the palate, it is cool and sweet, with light plum notes and just a hint of maple syrup sweetness. Light on the finish, it has a long lingering note of dark fruit, with just a touch of dry tannins at the end. Cascadia Rye is finished in port barrels, which layers a nice fruity character over the rye. At only two years old, the whiskey does not show any signs of youth or poor barrel management. If you are looking for a soft and fruity version of a rye whiskey, this should be at the top of your list. Sip neat or use in a fruitier Old-Fashioned.

Above: Cadée Cascadia Rye Whiskey Finished in Port Barrels.

Hotel Tango Distillery,
Indianapolis, IN

Lawrenceburg, IN 39° 05' 52.3" N, 84° 51' 38.3" W

Travis and Hilary Barnes founded the Hotel Tango Distillery in 2014. For a couple of years previously, Travis had been learning how to make whiskey, and they built their company using the 'same rigour, precision and

unwavering commitment' that Travis was schooled in during his service in the US Marine Corps. Barnes enlisted not long after the terrorist attacks that occurred on 11 September 2001 and learned how to be a leader serving three tours in Iraq. Hotel Tango gets its name from the influence of his military service, and its initials stand for Hilary and Travis. Today the distillery produces several spirits including vodka, gin, rum, liqueurs and whiskeys. And while they are distilling and ageing their own whiskeys, they also source, blend and bottle bourbon and rye from a couple of other distilleries. For their rye, the obvious choice was MGP in Lawrenceburg, with Rye, Ready-To-Drink being a two-year-old expression of MGP's 95% rye.

Above: Whiskey barrel being filled with new make spirit at Hotel Tango Distillery, Indianapolis, Indiana.

WHISKEYS

MASH BILL: 95% RYE, 5% BARLEY

Hotel Tango Rye, Ready-To-Drink Straight Rye Whiskey 50% ABV (100 proof)

Hotel Tango Rye, Ready-To-Drink Straight Rye Whiskey

50% ABV (100 proof)

On the nose, there is a herbaceous mix of mint, fennel and rye grain, with just a faint hint of oak. On the palate, it is lightly sweet, fruity and herbal, with notes of plum sprinkled with sugar, followed by fresh mint and a touch of rye bread. The finish is long and shows lots of great rye spice character, with a little residual heat from the whiskey. Overall, a very nice grain-forward rye whiskey. For those who like a little power in their whiskey, drink it neat, but for those who want something a little tamer, a touch of water or an ice cube will soften things. It will also serve well in several classic rye cocktails.

Above: Hotel Tango Rye, Ready-To-Drink Straight Rye Whiskey.

Templeton Rye Spirits, Templeton, IA

Lawrenceburg, IN 39° 05' 52.3" N, 84° 51' 38.3" W

In 2006, Meryl Kerkhoff, his son Keith and Scott Bush released their first batch of Templeton Rye whiskey. During Prohibition, Meryl's father Alphons Kerkhoff was a moonshiner in Templeton, Iowa, who made rye-flavoured rum by distilling a sugar wash with a little grain, which was (and still is) a common practice for moonshiners. Templeton has consistently claimed that its 21st-century whiskey was based on Alphons's recipe but there is no way this could be strictly true since what Alphons made was flavoured rum, yet Templeton sells whiskey. In 2014, the *Des Moines Register* and others began to seriously question some of Templeton's marketing materials and statements on its Tax and Trade Bureau (TTB)-approved label. In the end, Templeton confirmed that its whiskey has never been made from Alphons's recipe. Instead, it sources rye whiskey from MGP, made from its 95% rye mash bill, and blends the whiskey with a proprietary flavouring compound created by Clarendon Flavor Engineering in Louisville, Kentucky. The end result is then proofed and bottled. Given Templeton's growing sales, it is obvious that it created a product that people liked, so it seems odd that it chose to obscure the real provenance of its whiskey for so long. That same year, Templeton committed to updating its labels to include the required statement indicating that the base whiskey was distilled in Indiana, not Iowa, and removed references to a Prohibition-era recipe. Shortly after this, three class-action lawsuits were filed against Templeton claiming it had deceived customers and, in 2015, it settled the suits with a fund that capped its liability at $2.5 million (£1.8 million). The next year, Templeton announced a massive distillery expansion that ended up costing $35 million (£25.6 million) and began distilling new make rye in 2018, with its first bottles of Iowa-distilled Templeton expected in 2022.

WHISKEYS

MASH BILL: 95% RYE, 5% MALTED BARLEY

Templeton Rye Whiskey
– **Aged 4 Years** 40% ABV (80 proof)
– **Aged 6 Years** 45.75% ABV (91.5 proof)
– **Maple Cask Finish** 46% ABV (92 proof)
– **Barrel Strength** 57.9% ABV (115.8 proof)

IF YOU TRY ONE...

Templeton Rye Whiskey Aged 4 Years
40% ABV (80 proof)

The nose has light notes of fruit and spice like a sweet cherry cobbler. On the palate, the whiskey has a distinct sweetness that starts with caramel and cherry syrup and is followed by a bit of oak and cinnamon spice. Oak tannins slowly take over as the whiskey lingers on the tongue with just a hint of the initial fruity sweetness. Despite its extremely high rye content Templeton Rye tastes much sweeter than other examples. This is probably due to whatever harmless colouring, flavouring, or blending materials Templeton adds to the aged whiskey, which is why its label does not read as straight rye. Technicalities aside, its sweet and spicy profile has clearly found an enthusiastic public and Templeton can easily be enjoyed neat or in classic drinks such as an Old-Fashioned or Manhattan.

Above: Templeton Rye Whiskey Aged 4 Years.

Starlight Distillery

Borden, IN 38° 25' 21.8" N, 85° 55' 43.5" W

In 2001, Ted and Dana Huber founded the Starlight Distillery as an add-on to their Huber Orchard and Winery. The Hubers first established their Indiana farm in 1843, and for seven generations they have worked the land in southern Indiana. And for more than four decades, they have also had their finger on the pulse of American craft beverages. They established their winery in 1978 just two years after the Judgement of Paris rocked the wine world and demonstrated the excellence of American-made wine. Similarly, the Hubers were at the leading edge of the craft distilling movement, using their own fruit to make brandy. Three years after opening their distillery, their first brandy had reached maturity and was ready for sale. Over the next decade, the Hubers continued to make brandy and after a change in Indiana state law they were able to expand into distilling other spirits, releasing a vodka and gin while they distilled and matured bourbon and rye whiskey.

Above: Huber's Old Rickhouse Indiana Straight Rye Whiskey.

WHISKEYS

MASH BILL: 85% RYE, 15% MALTED BARLEY

Huber's Old Rickhouse Indiana Straight Rye Whiskey 46% ABV (92 proof)

IF YOU TRY ONE...

Huber's Old Rickhouse Indiana Straight Rye Whiskey
46% ABV (92 proof)

An intriguing aroma that is simultaneously fruity and herbaceous, with notes of fresh cherries, stone fruit, spruce tips and mint tea layered with oak. The first sip is sweet and then the oak comes in to balance things out. The flavours are a mixture of molasses, dark rye bread, tobacco, spearmint and oak, with light tannins to complement the sweetness. There is a lovely finish that blossoms with oak, rye bread and sweet mint tea. Overall, a particularly good rye whiskey that shows balance and lovely nuance of flavour. Enjoy neat, and it would pair nicely with a good cigar or pipe.

18th Street Distillery

Hammond, IN 41° 36' 54.4" N, 87° 31' 02.7" W

Drew Fox founded the Hammond-based 18th Street Distillery in 2018, one of the very few black-owned distilleries in the United States. But while Fox may be a relative newcomer to making spirits, he has also been a successful brewer for over a decade. Fox opened a small brewery in 2010, but within four years it quickly grew, producing more than 12,000 barrels of beer a year. As with many other start-up distilleries, Fox began by selling white spirits while his whiskeys aged. His rye whiskey is fermented, distilled, aged and bottled in-house, and has just reached the two-year mark. In 2020, Fox's Two Year Straight Bourbon earned a Double Gold medal and was named Best Craft Bourbon at the American Distilling Institute's Judging of Craft Spirits.

WHISKEYS

MASH BILL: RYE, CORN, MALTED BARLEY

18th Street Distillery Rye Whiskey 50% ABV (100 proof)

IF YOU TRY ONE...

18th Street Distillery Rye Whiskey 50% ABV (100 proof)

On the nose, there are notes of black tea, maple syrup and rye bread, plus a strong element of oak. On the palate, it is slightly hot and dry on the tongue, with lots of rye and spice notes, followed by a touch of young wood and red fruit. On the finish, it is soft and sweet with notes of black iced tea, honey and a light oak bite from the barrel. This is a nice whiskey that shows some signs of youth, but if you are drinking it on the rocks or in a mixed drink, you just won't notice.

Above: 18th Street Distillery Rye Whiskey.

Created by Jason Foust from the North End BBQ in Indianapolis, Hoosier Heritage was selected in 2015 by the Indiana State Museum's Cocktail Contest to be the unofficial state cocktail. Foust created the drink in honour of Abraham Lincoln, who moved to Indiana in 1816 from his family farm in central Kentucky.

Hoosier Heritage

MAKES 1

1 **rosemary sprig**

15ml (½fl oz) **maple syrup**

45ml (1½fl oz) **rye whiskey**

30ml (1fl oz) **unfiltered apple juice**

15ml (½fl oz) **lemon juice**

apple wheel or **cayenne pepper**, to garnish

Muddle the rosemary with the maple syrup in the bottom of a cocktail shaker. Add the remaining ingredients with ice and shake well. Double strain into an Old-Fashioned glass filled with ice. Garnish with an apple wheel, or sprinkle with cayenne pepper if you prefer a spicy kick.

Maryland
Rye whiskey

Both before and after National Prohibition, Maryland rye whiskey was one of the better-known regional styles of American whiskey. But as rye whiskey sales flatlined in the 1970s, the memory of Maryland rye all but disappeared from the national consciousness. Then in the early 2000s, drink historians and bartenders began to piece together the history of the style, while Maryland distillers started making new expressions of their state's once coveted whiskey. By the numbers, Maryland rye whiskey is nowhere near as popular as it once was. But as the overall category grows and the distribution of true Maryland rye continues to spread, whiskey drinkers will taste what this important regional American whiskey style has to offer.

History

Opposite: Widewater, part of the Chesapeake and Ohio (C&O) Canal below the Great Falls near Potomac, Maryland.

The first distiller of Maryland rye is probably lost to history, but given the geography of the region, distillers in and around the state were making rye whiskey that was softened somewhat by the addition of corn. In 1796, one

Climatic conditions: Frederick, MD – 8 active distilleries

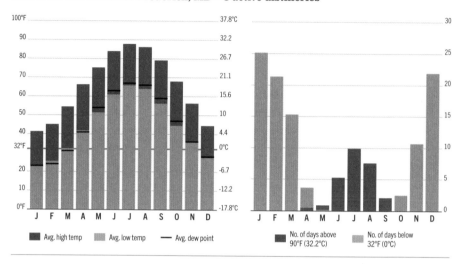

Avg. high temp   Avg. low temp   — Avg. dew point

No. of days above 90°F (32.2°C)   No. of days below 32°F (0°C)

year before George Washington ventured into distilling (see page 16), Baltimore's first business directory listed four distilleries operating in the city. In the period before the American Civil War, distilleries proliferated throughout the state including one built by William Lanahan, Sr, who sold Hunter Pure Rye (later renamed Hunter Baltimore Rye). After the war, popularity of Maryland rye spread across the nation, with brands like Hunter, Monticello Pure Rye, Mount Vernon Pure Rye, Orient Pure Rye and Sherwood Rye Whiskey becoming established nationally. Hunter was so successful that it was even exported to London, Shanghai and Manila.

Region Name:	State of Maryland
Nickname:	The Old Line State and the Free State
Capital City:	Annapolis
Population:	6,045,680
Number of Active Distilleries:	32
Whiskey Fact:	While most Maryland rye whiskey was made in and around Baltimore, MD, there have also been distillers in Delaware, DC, and Northern Virginia producing rye whiskey in the same ways, making it more of a regional style than one bounded by state borders.

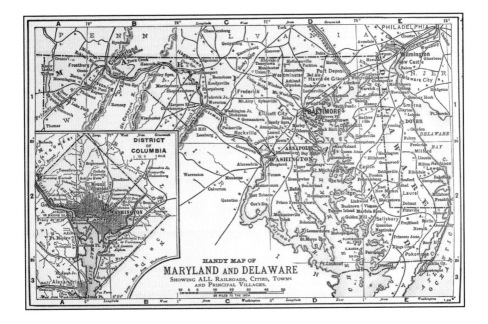

One possible explanation for the popularity of Maryland rye is the American Civil War itself. During the war, huge numbers of Union and Confederate soldiers criss-crossed the state. President Abraham Lincoln was determined to protect Washington DC and Baltimore from the Confederates. So as the Union Army of the Potomac moved south in its attempts to capture Richmond, Virginia (capital of the Confederacy), Lincoln made sure that DC was well guarded by fresh troops from the North. In addition, General Robert E Lee's Army of Northern Virginia twice crossed into western Maryland with the military goal of cutting off supply lines to DC and the practical goal of raiding farms and towns to resupply his army. It is certain that during these campaigns, local rye whiskey was among the goods looted by the Confederates. As both Union and Confederate soldiers converged in Maryland, it is very possible that some of them returned home with fond memories of the local whiskey.

   Another potential reason for the widespread fame of Maryland rye in the era before National Prohibition was the Centennial Exposition, hosted by Philadelphia, PA,

Above: An official map of Maryland (and Delaware), date unknown.

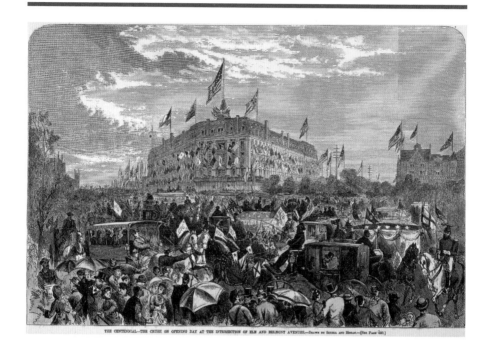

THE CENTENNIAL—THE CRUSH ON OPENING DAY AT THE INTERSECTION OF ELM AND BELMONT AVENUES—DRAWN BY SCHELL AND HOGAN.—[SEE PAGE 490.]

Above: Opening day of the Philadelphia Centennial Exposition, 19 May 1876.

in 1876 to commemorate the United States' 100th year of independence. At the exposition, various buildings were erected to celebrate and showcase the achievements of the country, including one for agriculture. The agriculture exhibit also happened to include a fully functional model distillery. Perhaps for its alleged connection to George Washington, the Baltimore-based Mount Vernon Distillery operated the centennial distillery and extolled the purity and quality of their rye whiskey. Over the course of 184 days from 10 May to 10 November 1876, almost 10 million visitors attended the exposition.

While it is uncertain if civil war, civil celebration or something else can explain the growing popularity of Maryland rye, National Prohibition helped to end it. From 1881 to 1912, whiskey production in Maryland grew from 2.4 million US gallons (9.1 million litres) to 5.6 million US gallons (21.2 million litres), with a total of 19.3 million US gallons (73 million litres) held in bonded warehouses. During this time, more popular brands such as Pikesville Rye (now distilled in Kentucky by Heaven Hill) and

Melvale Rye were introduced, with Melvale being one of the largest, with a daily mashing capacity of 1,000 bushels of grain (roughly 50,000lb/22,700kg). It was also at this time that the distillers invested considerable money in advertising the Maryland brand. Hunter Baltimore Rye displayed ads at baseball stadiums in Baltimore, New York and Chicago, while Sherwood Rye, Antietam Rye and Old Horsey Rye advertised their aged rye on ships that travelled from San Francisco to Cape Horn and back. But despite the popularity of Maryland rye among drinkers, the prohibition movement was stronger, and in 1920, American Medicinal Spirits Co. (AMS), which ran the Hannis Distilling Company in Baltimore, was the only distillery allowed to operate in the state, selling its Mount Vernon Rye as medicinal whiskey until Prohibition ended.

After Repeal, a small handful of Maryland distillers reopened, but most of them were short-lived due to the changing tastes of American drinkers. The Hannis Distillery, which National Distillers purchased near the end of National Prohibition, ran until 1953, when it closed because of lagging sales. Meanwhile, in Dundalk, William E Kricker built the Baltimore Pure Rye Distillery and sold bottled-in-bond rye made from 98% rye and only 2% malted barley, which was very unusual for the region. But for unknown reasons, Kricker sold the distillery in the early 1950s to National Distillers, who quickly closed it and sold the building to Seagram to make blended whiskeys (see

Above: Advertisement for Hunter Rye whiskey, 1906.

Left: Workers spilling seized beer during Prohibition.

page 122). Like Hannis, the Corporation Trust Corporation (CTC) purchased the rights to the old Monumental Distillery from Baltimore and relocated it to Lansdowne, Maryland. Monumental distilled and bottled its own brand of whiskey, but in 1936, Andrew W Merle, the new owner of Pikesville Rye, contracted CTC to make whiskey for him. In 1942, an accident at the distillery forced it to reincorporate as Majestic Distilling Company, though Pikesville continued to be made there in the same way. Finally, in 1972, Majestic, the last operating Maryland distillery at that time, filled its final barrel of Pikesville Rye. The brand continued to be bottled from its remaining stock for the next ten years when Heaven Hill purchased Pikesville in 1982, moved production to Bardstown, Kentucky, and lowered the rye content to the 51% legal minimum.

As across the nation, Maryland's first craft distilleries opened in the early 2000s. In 2005, the Maryland General Assembly passed a law allowing state wineries to produce up to 200 US gallons (757 litres) of spirits a year. But despite this significant restriction, Mike Fiore, owner of the Fiore Winery, was the first to receive a licence under the new law and became Maryland's first legal distiller in the state since 1972. Fiore was quickly followed in 2008 by Blackwater Distilling, and Lyon Distilling in 2012, which in 2014 released

Below: An early 1900s photograph of L Winand & Brothers Distillery, located north of Baltimore in Scott's Level, Maryland. This was the original home of Pikesville Maryland Rye Whiskey.

what may have been the first Maryland rye whiskey, though the company now focuses on rum. Since then, more than a dozen distilleries in Maryland, Delaware, Washington DC and Virginia have joined the pack, releasing their own versions of Maryland rye, making it more of a regional style than one bound by state borders. While many of these whiskeys are still young and have limited distribution, they have begun the work of restoring the pride and excellence that was, is and will be Maryland rye whiskey.

Production requirements

At present, there is no legal or industry-generated definition of Maryland rye whiskey. But it is increasingly accepted that one of its defining features is a mixed mash bill of about two-thirds rye and one-third other grains, often corn and malted barley. And while there are historical examples with different ratios and different grain combinations, this is a good starting point. Today, Maryland rye whiskey must meet the definitions of rye in the Federal Standards of Identity (51% rye – see page 124) and be made in Maryland. That said, the Alcohol and Tobacco Tax and Trade Bureau (TTB) has approved labels for 'Maryland-style' rye whiskeys produced outside the state, as far away as Colorado, though this book focuses on Maryland, and Maryland-adjacent rye whiskeys relevant to the history and geography of the region.

DELMARVA PENINSULA

Painted Stave Distilling

Smyrna, Delaware 39° 17' 58.1" N, 75° 36' 30.8" W

Ron Gomes and Mike Rasmussen met in 2011 when they were both independently exploring the idea of opening a distillery and a mutual friend introduced them to each other. Two years later they had renovated an old movie theatre to house their distillery and began making spirits. As with many craft distilleries, they started by selling vodka and gin while their whiskeys aged, which they first released in 2015. Their whiskey range includes corn whisky, bourbon, spirit distilled from beer, and rye.

WHISKEYS

MASH BILL: MARYLAND RYE MASH

Diamond State Straight Rye Whiskey 44% ABV (88 proof)

Diamond State 5th Anniversary Straight Rye Whiskey 44% ABV (88 proof) Finished in stout beer barrels.

Painted Stave Bottled in Bond Rye Whiskey 50% ABV (100 proof)

IF YOU TRY ONE...

Painted Stave Bottled in Bond Rye Whiskey

50% ABV (100 proof)

Above: Painted Stave Bottled in Bond Rye Whiskey.

With a somewhat muted aroma of apple cider layered with oak, caramel and just a touch of wood smoke, on the palate it is semi-dry with a good dose of oak tannins mixed with corn sweetness so as not to be overwhelming. There are flavours of grassy rye, dried mint leaves, sarsaparilla, vanilla and molasses, followed on the finish with lots of warm rye and baking spice notes that softly open to baked apple and caramel. Overall, it has a great rye character while being a bit powerful in wood flavours and the alcohol. One for those who tend towards more

woody bourbons, it can be enjoyed in any of the usual ways: neat, on the rocks or in a cocktail. Given its sarsaparilla character, this would be a good whiskey substitute in a Bourbon Lift, usually made with whiskey, orgeat syrup, double cream, coffee liqueur and sparkling water.

Above: Old Smyrna Theater, home of Painted Stave Distilling, Smyrna, Delaware.

CENTRAL MARYLAND

Baltimore Spirits Company

Baltimore, MD 39° 20' 10.1" N, 76° 38' 40.0" W

Max Lents, Eli Breitburg-Smith and Ian Newton founded the Baltimore Whiskey Company in 2015, in the Remington district of Baltimore. They quickly began distilling rye whiskey and laying it down to age while they sold other spirits like their gin, smoked apple brandy, amaro and others. Two years later they moved to a new location, having outgrown their original space, and renamed the business as the Baltimore Spirits Company, better reflecting their wider range of spirits. Finally, in 2018 they began releasing their Epoch Rye, which was distilled from a mash of 70% rye and 30% malted rye on a still modelled after the Lagavulin stills in Islay, Scotland.

MASH BILL: 70% RYE, 30% MALTED RYE

Baltimore Epoch Straight Rye Whiskey 50% ABV (100 proof)

Baltimore Epoch Bottled-In-Bond Straight Rye Whiskey
50% ABV (100 proof)

IF YOU TRY ONE...

Baltimore Epoch Straight Rye Whiskey
50% ABV (100 proof)

Above: Baltimore Epoch Straight Rye Whiskey.

First aromas are green wood, alcohol, grape skins and stems, but as the whiskey breathes and opens, sweeter notes of honey, biscuits and roses start to emerge, combined with grape juice and cloves. On the palate, the whiskey has an interesting combination of flavours that include milk chocolate, orange zest, rye grain, pumpernickel bread and a touch of aniseed that cools the tongue. The finish starts somewhat hot, though that quickly fades and leaves a lingering flavour of young wood, fruit and a light and not off-putting astringency. At two years old, Epoch is still a young whiskey, but it shows good care and attention in its distillation and ageing. As it opens, the initial greenness fades and reveals a decent whiskey with exciting potential for future releases as it continues to mature. Drink neat, on the rocks or in your preferred cocktail.

CAPITAL

McClintock Distilling Company

Frederick, MD 39° 24' 47.1" N, 77° 24' 30.3" W

Braeden Bumpers and Tyler Hegamyer co-founded McClintock Distilling in 2013, and after years of work opened their distillery on 3 December 2016. The distillery is named after a local inventor, McClintock Young, who envisioned Frederick becoming 'a hub for manufacturing, commerce and culture'. McClintock began by selling vodka, gin and white whiskey with barrels of their new make bourbon and rye aged in barrels. Since opening, McClintock has committed to using organic ingredients, and in January 2018, they became the first Maryland distillery to be certified organic by the United States Department of Agriculture (USDA). True to fashion, McClintock's rye whiskey is made from heirloom varietals of rye, red wheat and corn, which are stoneground by a historic mill nearby.

WHISKEYS

MASH BILL: 75% RYE, 20% RED WHEAT AND 5% CORN

McClintock Distilling Bootjack Rye Whiskey 45% ABV (90 proof)

McClintock Distilling Maryland Heritage White Whiskey
42% ABV (84 proof) New make rye stored for 24 hours in charred new oak casks before bottling.

IF YOU TRY ONE...

McClintock Distilling Bootjack Rye Whiskey
45% ABV (90 proof)

A lovely aroma of dark pumpernickel, with just a hint of raisin sweetness, on the palate it is warm and inviting, with a pleasant spice character mixed with a light sweetness that tastes of dates and prunes. The finish has a slightly odd flavour like sourdough starter and fennel, which dissipates and evolves into warm fruit, spice and oak flavours.

Above: McClintock Distilling Bootjack Rye Whiskey.

Below: McClintock Distilling Company, Frederick, Maryland.

The Diamondback cocktail first appeared in *Ted Saucier's Bottoms Up* in 1951, though it is likely that the drink predates the book by a couple of decades. While the drink took its name from the Diamondback Lounge, formerly located inside the Lord Baltimore Hotel in Baltimore, the lounge was named after the diamondback terrapin. These turtles are endemic to the Chesapeake Bay and are found in the brackish waters of the eastern United States, as far north as Cape Cod and as far south as the Florida Keys. In 1932, the University of Maryland adopted the diamondback terrapin as its mascot.

Diamondback

MAKES 1

45ml (1½fl oz) **rye whiskey**

22ml (¾fl oz) **apple brandy**

22ml (¾fl oz) **Yellow Chartreuse**

Add all the ingredients to a cocktail shaker with ice. Shake well until cold, then strain over a large ice cube in an Old-Fashioned glass.

Pennsylvania
Rye whiskey

In the story of American history, Pennsylvania distillers burst on to the scene in 1791 only to fade away three years later. And yet, through their whiskey, Pennsylvania distillers have helped shape American drinking culture and influence the taste preferences of several generations of Americans. For more than a century, Pennsylvania rye whiskey, often referred to as Old Monongahela (pronounced MO-non-gah-HEEL-a), was a hugely popular style of regional American whiskey, second only to Kentucky bourbon. Changing tastes in the drinking public spelled the demise of the style. But just two decades later, renewed interest in rye whiskey generally helped to resurrect this past icon of regional American whiskey.

History

Quite a bit of what we know about Pennsylvania distilleries from the 1850s onwards is due to a German immigrant, surveyor and map-maker named Ernest Hexamer, who used his skills to create detailed surveys of cities, businesses

Opposite: Farmland in Lancaster County, Pennsylvania.

Climatic conditions: Pittsburgh, PA – 7 active distilleries

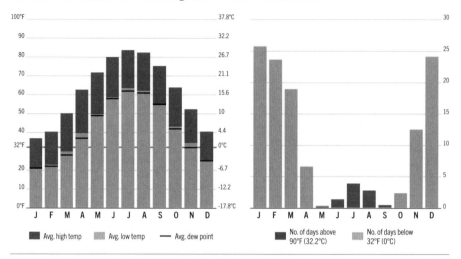

Avg. high temp   ▨ Avg. low temp   — Avg. dew point

No. of days above 90°F (32.2°C)   No. of days below 32°F (0°C)

and manufacturing plants for insurance companies. For distilleries, Hexamer recorded all sorts of details such as the type of whiskey they produced, what grains they used, the type and volume of stills used and which buildings were heated. Looking at distillers across the state, a few interesting similarities pop up. First, for most of the distilleries Hexamer surveyed, rye whiskey was the primary or sole spirit they sold. Second, most of that rye whiskey was made from a two-grain mash of rye and malted barley, though a couple included malted rye or wheat and only one included corn. Third, many of them used a wooden still for their stripping run (the first distillation where the alcohol is stripped from the fermented mash) and a copper still for their spirit run (the second distillation where the distiller collects the portion of the spirit that contains the alcohol and flavours they want), though there were a couple that used what was probably a wooden Coffey still that fed spirit to a copper doubler (a pot still that further refines the spirit and allows it to reach its full strength). Lastly, most of the bonded warehouses were equipped with steam pipes for heating the buildings. In one description, Hexamer notes that the heat in the barrel house was 'moderate' because it stayed below 80°F (26.7°C)!

Region Name:	Commonwealth of Pennsylvania
Nickname:	The Keystone State
Capital City:	Harrisburg
Population:	12,801,989
Number of Active Distilleries:	93
Whiskey Fact:	Pre-Prohibition Pennsylvania distilleries were known for using steam-fed pipes to heat their barrel warehouses from the mid-70s°F (24°C) to as high as 100°F (38°C).

Before the Bottled-in-Bond Act of 1897 (see page 19), many of these Pennsylvania distillers were selling their rye by the barrel to more distant clients in places like Illinois and Missouri, who would blend and bottle it. But for closer markets such as Pittsburgh, Philadelphia, New York and others, their ryes were sold by the bottle under brands such as Dougherty's, Kinsey, W.W.W. Rye, Philadelphia Pure, Pennsylvania Club, Wheatland (which had no wheat), Gibson's, Guckenheimer, Montrose, Old Bridgeport and Old Overholt.

Below: An official map of Pennsylvania, drawn in 1883.

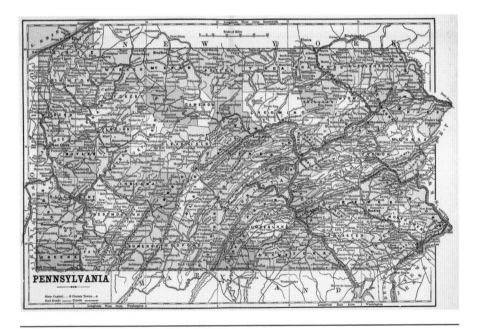

Above: Old Overholt Straight Rye Whiskey.

Around 1919, distilleries throughout the state began to close in anticipation of National Prohibition. One exception was A. Overholt & Co., which at that point had been in operation for almost 110 years. That same year, Henry Clay Frick, the last remaining heir of the Overholt holdings, willed the company and its two distilleries in Western Pennsylvania to his friend Andrew Mellon. Mellon was politically connected, so when Warren Harding was elected president in 1920, Mellon was selected to serve as the then new Secretary of the Treasury. Not surprisingly, Overholt happened to be one of the few distilleries that applied and received a licence from the Treasury to sell medicinal whiskey during Prohibition. There was an outcry from the press and prohibitionists at the Secretary's direct connection to selling whiskey and so Mellon sold Overholt to the Union Trust Company. And it just so happened that Mellon was one of Union's board of directors. However, in 1925 Overholt was sold to the New York-based grocer Park & Tilford, who operated the distillery until 1932.

After Prohibition, Park & Tilford sold the Overholt distilleries to the new National Distillers Products Co., which was quickly snatching up brands, distilleries and whiskey stocks around the country. Along with Old Grand-Dad Bourbon (see page 52), Old Taylor Bourbon and Mount Vernon Rye, Old Overholt Rye became one of National Distillers' top brands after Prohibition. National sold Old Overholt as a four-year-old bottled-in-bond rye just as it was before Prohibition. A mere ten years after Repeal, national whiskey sales were booming, but the age statement on Old Overholt started to creep up slowly from four years, to five, six and then seven years. According to US law, the age statement must state the age of the youngest spirit in the bottle. Given that Overholt had sold most, if not all, of its pre-Prohibition whiskey, this increasing age statement indicates that they were producing way more whiskey than they were selling, and it was steadily getting older.

As the decades wore on, sales of rye whiskey continued to decline, reaching its nadir in the early 2000s. Eventually, both National Distillers and Continental Distilling Corporation, owner of Rittenhouse Rye, were forced to close and some of their assets were sold off. Heaven Hill purchased Rittenhouse around 1983, and Jim Beam (see page 52) picked up Old Overholt and Old

Below: Metal strainer catching chunks of charred wood as rye whiskey is dumped into a tank at Mountain Laurel Spirits, Bristol, Pennsylvania.

Above: Magazine advertisement for Philadelphia Blended Whisky, 1947.

Grand-Dad from National in 1987. While Beam added the Old Grand-Dad bourbon mash to its production schedule, both Beam and Heaven Hill scrapped the original Pennsylvania rye recipes and made them in the Kentucky style of 51% rye, temporarily ending the more than two-hundred-year history of Pennsylvania rye whiskey.

But after a near three-decade hiatus, Pennsylvania craft distillers reintroduced the nation to their eponymous rye. Herman Mihalich and John Cooper founded Mountain Laurel Spirits in 2011 (see opposite), making the first Pennsylvania rye whiskey for over 20 years. And they were quickly followed by the Pittsburgh Distilling Company, who released their Wigle Pennsylvania Rye (see page 161). Since then, more distilleries have opened around the state and many of them have chosen to create their own versions of Pennsylvania rye, helping bit by bit to build a new legacy for this important regional style of American whiskey.

Production requirements

Currently there is no legal or industry standard for Pennsylvania rye whiskey beyond those set out in the Federal Standards of Identity for rye and the requirement that the whiskey be produced in the Keystone State. Historical records show that the Pennsylvania rye so many loved was distilled from a mash roughly comprised of 75% rye and 25% other grains like malted barley, malted rye or wheat. Although almost all the contemporary Pennsylvania ryes have adopted this model for their mash bills, there do not seem to be any that use wooden stills or age their barrels in heated warehouses as their forerunners did. However, for today's Pennsylvania distillers interested in crafting their own expressions of rye, the current federal framework leaves plenty of room for them to be creative, while adopting some of the historical practices that made whiskey from the state so famous.

PHILADELPHIA

Mountain Laurel Spirits

Bristol, PA 40° 06' 13.9" N, 74° 51' 06.9" W

Herman Mihalich and John Cooper founded Mountain Laurel Spirits in 2011 with the single goal of making Pennsylvania rye whiskey. Mihalich grew up living above the bar his family owned in Monessen, and in 2006, after reading about the revival of American rye whiskey, he was inspired to make his own. Their brand name Dad's Hat harks back to Mihalich's fond memories of his dad who always wore a hat when he left the house and particularly liked Stetson fedoras made in Philadelphia. Much of their grain is sourced from local farmers and

Below: Founders of Mountain Laurel Spirits, John Cooper (left) and Herman Mihalich (right).

their mash includes a mixture of 80% rye, 15% malted barley and 5% malted rye. After fermenting for about a week, the mash is double distilled before going into charred new oak barrels. Their Classic Rye is aged for six months in quarter casks, while all their older whiskeys go into full-sized 53-US-gallon (200-litre) barrels. In 2015, *Whiskey Advocate* named Dad's Hat Pennsylvania Rye its Craft Whiskey of the Year.

WHISKEYS

MASH BILL: 80% RYE, 15% MALTED BARLEY, 5% MALTED RYE

Dad's Hat Pennsylvania Rye Whiskey
- **Classic Rye** 45% ABV (90 Proof)
- **Straight Rye** 47.5% ABV (95 Proof)
- **Bottled in Bond** 50% ABV (100 Proof)
- **Finished in Vermouth Barrels** 47% ABV (94 Proof)
- **Finished in Port Wine Barrels** 47% ABV (94 Proof)

Above: Dad's Hat Pennsylvania Straight Rye Whiskey.

IF YOU TRY ONE...

Dad's Hat Pennsylvania Straight Rye Whiskey

47.5% (95 proof)

On the nose, there is an inviting aroma of fresh baked rye bread, molasses, a light grassy note from the malted rye and just a hint of liquorice. As the whiskey sits, more fruit aromas of fresh cherry, plum and nectarine meet your nose. On the palate, similar flavours carry over on to the tongue with notes of toasted rye bread spread with a thin layer of salted butter, followed by tobacco, dried peach, cherry, a hint of caramel and a pleasant grassy character. After swallowing, it has a long, warm finish that lingers with notes of fennel, rye, dried mint and stone fruit. The combination of the alcohol and the subtle mintiness gives it a slight menthol tingling sensation on your lips that brings you back for another sip. This delicious whiskey is a great example of both Pennsylvania rye and the judicious use of malted rye. While some rye drinkers familiar with those made in Kentucky or Indiana may be thrown off by the distinct vegetal character of malted rye, Dad's Hat is a good introduction, and after a few drinks one quickly becomes enamoured with its complexity.

Above: Three stills and other equipment at Conneaut Cellars Winery & Distillery, Conneaut Lake, Pennsylvania.

Conneaut Cellars Winery & Distillery

Conneaut Lake, PA 41° 36' 06.9" N, 80° 17' 50.4" W

Dr Alan Wolf founded Conneaut Cellars Winery in 1982 after studying winemaking in Germany. His son Joal Wolf worked a full career in the US military before joining his father at the winery in 1988, eventually becoming wine master and then the owner in 1996. The winery went on to win numerous awards, and in 2013, Joal decided to add on a distillery. Today they make brandy, vodka, rum, coffee liqueur, bourbon and rye whiskey. For their rye, they have resurrected the old Meadville Distilling Co. rye brand, distilled from a traditional Monongahela-style rye, which presumably means lots of rye, some malted barley and no corn.

MASH BILL: UNDISCLOSED

Meadville Pure Rye Whiskey 50% ABV (100 Proof)

IF YOU TRY ONE...

Meadville Pure Rye Whiskey

50% ABV (100 proof)

The nose is bright and fruity with notes of green apple, fresh plum and nectarine, layered underneath with notes of sweet cherries and toasted oak. On the palate, it has a stronger wood character without being overwhelming, supported by notes of rye grain and a hint of sweetness. On the finish, it is hot and light with flavours of rose petals, plum skins and wood. A very solid rye whiskey that shows light fruity flavours combined nicely with wood and spice notes common in rye. At 50% ABV, the whiskey is a little hot, but a touch of water or an ice cube would work well to tame the heat and reveal more flavour. It would also make a very good Manhattan.

Above: Meadville Pure Rye Whiskey.

PITTSBURGH

Pittsburgh Distilling Company

Pittsburgh, PA 40° 27' 15.6" N, 79° 58 '52.8" W

The Meyer and Grelli families founded the Pittsburgh Distilling Company in 2010, which became operational in 2011 and opened to the public in March 2012. Since then, the company has expanded to make a staggering number of liqueurs, rums, bottled cocktails and a few other spirits, with its core focus on whiskey. The Wigle brand is named after Philip Wigle, a Pennsylvania farmer who was convicted of treason for his role in the Whiskey Rebellion (see page 13) and sentenced to hang, though he was later pardoned by President Washington. Meanwhile, Pittsburgh Distilling has set for itself the mission to build community around their distillery, supporting local agriculture and creating jobs by producing innovative and terroir-focused spirits entirely within Pittsburgh.

For their rye whiskeys, they pot distill a mash of locally sourced organic rye and wheat grown in Western Pennsylvania. The new make is then aged two to four years in a combination of 25- and 53-US-gallon (95- and 200-litre) charred new oak barrels. Their whiskeys have won multiple awards, and in 2018 and 2019, their Pennsylvania Straight Rye was a James Beard Awards Semi-Finalist.

WHISKEYS

MASH BILL: 68% REGIONAL ORGANIC RYE, 18% REGIONAL ORGANIC WHEAT, 14% ORGANIC MALTED BARLEY

Wigle Straight Rye Whiskey
– **Pennsylvania** 42% ABV (84 Proof)
– **Suffragette** 42% ABV (84 Proof)
– **Single Barrel** 50% ABV (100 Proof)
– **Deep Cut** 60% ABV (120 Proof)

MASH BILL: MALTED RYE, MALTED BARLEY

Wigle Kilted Malted Rye Whiskey Finished in Scotch Whisky Casks 46% ABV (92 Proof) Finished in used Laphroaig Quarter Casks.

IF YOU TRY ONE...

Wigle Pennsylvania Straight Rye Whiskey
42% ABV (84 proof)

Very fruity on the nose with notes of bubblegum and white peach, plus a touch of vanilla, on the palate it is semi-sweet with flavours of tart cherry, oak, black pepper and cinnamon. On the finish, it turns to darker notes of tobacco, nutmeg and clove, with a light hint of sweet mint and cinnamon candies. This is a good example of rye whiskey made without corn. The majority of the fruit and sweetness comes from esters formed during fermentation and wood sugars extracted during ageing. At 42% ABV, the alcohol is soft on the palate, but the flavour overall is very robust. It would work well neat, paired with a cigar, and it works nicely in cocktails with sweet vermouth.

Above: Wigle Pennsylvania Straight Rye Whiskey.

Quantum Spirits

Carnegie, PA 40° 24' 31.2" N, 80° 05' 04.4" W

In 2018, Ryan and Sarah Kanto opened their Quantum Spirits distillery inside the old Steinmetz Bakery in Carnegie. Ryan is an engineer by training, and he and Sarah quickly brought in Chris McNary, who received a Ph.D. from the University of Utah as a chemical physicist, to run their lab and assist with distilling. With a heavy science background, they have made it their mission to make spirits through a process of innovation using 'new technology, new methods and new ingredients'. Quantum began by releasing vodka, gin and liqueurs while they were ageing their rye whiskey using the Spanish solera system. Their first rye whiskey release, which they dubbed Copper Edition, came from

Below: Digital system tracking temperature pressure sensor data at Quantum Spirits, Carnegie, Pennsylvania.

the first layer of the solera, with future releases to come from the middle layer with more ageing time in the form of the Silver Edition and then the final layer of the solera with the most age in a Gold Edition.

WHISKEYS

MASH BILL: RYE, MALTED RYE

Quantum Spirits Solera Rye Whiskey Finished in American Oak 47% ABV (94 proof)
– Copper Edition
– Silver Edition
– Gold Edition

Above: Quantum Spirits Copper Edition Solera Rye Whiskey Finished in American Oak.

IF YOU TRY ONE...

Quantum Spirits Copper Edition Solera Rye Whiskey Finished in American Oak 47% ABV (94 proof)

The nose explodes with sweet aromas of vanilla, caramel and soft butterscotch chews. Underneath the sweet aromas is a slight grassy and spice note from the rye and malt. On the palate, the grassy note from the rye malt comes through first, quickly followed by a slight spice character and then sweet caramel and vanilla come crashing in. After the second sip, the sweetness begins to dissipate and more of the rye malt grassiness shines through. On the finish, it maintains a similar profile of grassy malted rye and caramel, with an added note of bright green apple. The grassy sweet flavour is somewhat reminiscent of an añejo tequila. For fans of rye who enjoy the grassy flavours of malted rye and want a whiskey with more sweetness, look for Quantum.

At the turn of the 20th century, McKeesport, Pennsylvania had an active cocktail scene that, for a few decades, had a significant impact on US drinking culture. South of Pittsburgh, McKeesport helped popularize the term 'speakeasy' and was home to the Fussfungle, a cocktail made from 'pure spirits, water, burnt brown sugar and molasses'. The drink spread west to Topeka, Kansas and east to New York, and word of it went as far as Honolulu, Hawaii. While there do not seem to be any surviving recipes for how the drink was originally made, Sean Enright, general manager at Spork, an upscale restaurant in East Liberty, Pittsburgh, created the modern interpretation from which the following recipe has been adapted.

Fussfungle

MAKES 1

15ml (½fl oz) **Burnt Brown Sugar and Molasses Syrup** (see below)

60ml (2fl oz) **rye whiskey**

orange peel, to garnish

FOR THE BURNT BROWN SUGAR AND MOLASSES SYRUP

110g (4oz) **brown sugar**

120ml (4fl oz) **hot water**

70g (2½oz) **molasses**

Fill a mixing glass with ice, add the Burnt Brown Sugar and Molasses Syrup and then the whiskey and stir until very cold. Strain into an Old-Fashioned glass with a large ice cube and garnish with an orange peel.

To make the Burnt Brown Sugar and Molasses Syrup, heat the brown sugar in a saucepan until the sugar melts and begins to bubble. Remove from the heat, add the hot water and stir until the sugar is fully dissolved. Then add the molasses and stir until fully incorporated. Allow to cool, then pour into a clean bottle or jar and seal. The syrup may be stored in the refrigerator for up to a month.

New York
Empire Rye whiskey

Both the city and state of New York have played an important role in the development of America's drinking culture. During the 1880s and early 2000s, New York bars were setting trends in cocktails and bar culture that spread throughout the country. Before Prohibition, rye whiskey flowed throughout the state – part of the reason why so many classic cocktails called for its use – and NY's influence has also been blamed by some elitists for popularizing 'inferior' drinks such as the Gin Rickey and the Cosmopolitan. But while the influence of New York bars has been well documented, its distilleries have received less coverage. Today's New York distillers deserve credit for challenging the idea that American whiskey is Kentucky and Tennessee versus everything else, having played an important role in reinvigorating the idea among the press and the drinking public that regional styles of American whiskey can be just as relevant today as they were in the 1800s.

Opposite: New York's iconic Chrysler Building.

Climatic conditions: Brooklyn, NY – 13 active distilleries

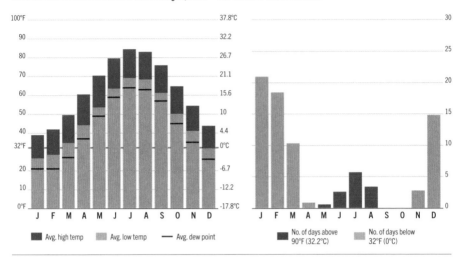

Avg. high temp ▮   Avg. low temp ▨   — Avg. dew point

No. of days above 90°F (32.2°C) ▮   No. of days below 32°F (0°C) ▨

History

In 1621, the Dutch West India Company (GWC) established the New Netherlands colony, which stretched along the east coast of North America from what is today Delaware to Cape Cod in Massachusetts. Three years later, it sponsored 30 families to settle in New Amsterdam (Manhattan) to serve as a tactical and trading outpost for its rapidly growing colony. By 1640, Willem Kieft, the director of the colony, ordered the construction of the first commercial distillery in North America on Staten Island. It is thought that it produced apple brandy, rum and a version of genever distilled from beer infused with hops and juniper berries.

Region Name:	State of New York
Nickname:	The Empire State
Capital City:	Albany
Population:	19,453,561
Number of Active Distilleries:	158
Whiskey Fact:	Craft distilleries in NY have gained several privileges, such as operating tasting rooms and limited direct-to-consumer sales by linking their spirits to state-grown agricultural products, because, while liquor may get a bad rap, farmers are as American as apple pie.

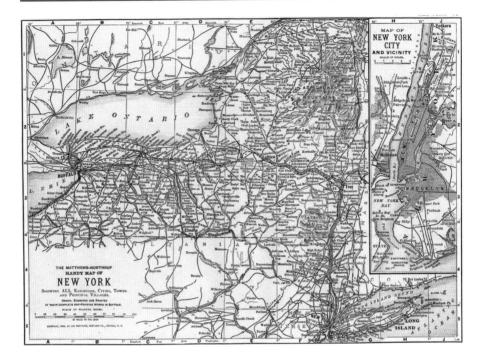

During the British colonial era up to 1765, American distillers in New York and New England produced huge volumes of rum due to the low cost of molasses imported as part of the Atlantic triangular slave trade (see page 12). However, after the American Revolution, the cost of molasses dramatically increased and the large export markets for rum in Europe and Africa were cut off. This led many distillers to focus on selling to their local and regional markets. Once the glut of cheap rum dried up, many Americans turned to rye whiskey to slake their thirst.

While the largest distillers of rye before Prohibition were in Pennsylvania and Maryland, at its peak, New York State had over 1,000 small distilleries making several spirits, including rye whiskey. However, Prohibition closed all the state's distilleries and they would not reopen until 2003. In 1933, when the 21st Amendment to the US Constitution both repealed Prohibition and gave the US states the power to regulate alcohol within their borders, there did not seem to be any interest in fostering

Above: An official map of New York, published in 1898.

Right: A well-stocked bar at Bill's Gay Nineties, a speakeasy located at 57 East 54th Street, New York City, c. 1940.

RYE GRAIN

Thought to be native to modern Turkey, rye grain is biologically related to both wheat and barley, and it is well adapted to growing in poor soils and tolerant to cold. Rye was  introduced to the Americas by Dutch and English settlers, and the grain quickly took root in the Mid-Atlantic and North Colonies, which tend to have very cold winters. Rye was an important commercial crop in the United States for the better part of two centuries, and reached its peak in 1919 with over 7 million acres (2.8 million hectares) harvested. The demand for rye then quickly fell, partly due to the end of wheat rationing imposed during World War I and the beginning of Prohibition, which proved to be the death knell for the large rye whiskey distillers in Pennsylvania and Maryland. Around 2000, rye cultivation had settled to about 2 million acres (810,000 hectares) with only about 275,000 of those acres (111,300 hectares) being harvested per year. The remaining acreage is planted as a cover crop to help hold the topsoil during the winter and can be tilled back into the ground to add nitrogen. However, the recent sales boom in rye whiskey has begun to increase the amount of rye harvested each year.

commercial distilling in New York. When the state rewrote its liquor laws, it added a licence for distillers that was so expensive that no one bothered to apply. However, in 2000, the state legislature added a micro-distillery licence for only $1,500, and three years later, Tuthilltown Spirits (see page 178) became the first New York distillery to open in 70 years. Then in 2007, New York Governor Andrew Cuomo pushed for a new law, the Farm Distillery Act, which further cut the licence for small distillers if they used 50 per cent state-grown agricultural products in their spirits. This pushed the growing number of small distillers in the state to work with local farmers to plant rye and the other grains they needed.

Above: Advertising label, Bininger's Traveler's Guide Bourbon, New York, 1859.

One late night in spring 2014, a group of New York distillers met for drinks in Denver, Colorado during the American Craft Spirits Association's inaugural convention to discuss the burgeoning industry in their state and how they might collectively promote the whiskeys they were making. Out of that meeting, they settled on the idea of creating a shared trademark for a new style of whiskey called Empire Rye. That same year, New York State would amend the Farm Distillery Act to give these small distillers more economic incentives while upping the requirement that their spirits use at least 75 per cent state-grown agricultural products. The following year, the Empire Rye Whiskey Association was founded. Today, there are at least 15 New York distilleries

Left: Logo of New York's Empire Rye Whiskey Association.

selling their versions of Empire Rye, with another dozen distilleries committed to releasing Empire Ryes in the coming years.

Production requirements

To qualify to use the moniker and logo of Empire Rye on a bottle of whiskey, the whiskey must conform to the following standard created by the Empire Rye Whiskey Association. It must be mashed, fermented, distilled, barrelled and aged at a single New York State licensed farm distiller from a mash that consists of at least 75% New York State-grown rye grain, which may be raw, malted or a combination of the two. The remainder can be composed of any other raw or malted grain, grown in or outside the state. The mash must be distilled to not more than 160 proof (80% ABV), aged for a minimum of two years in charred new oak barrels at not more than 115 proof (57.5% ABV) at the time of entry and bottled at no less than 80 proof (40% ABV). If a whiskey is made from combining 100% qualifying Empire Rye whiskeys from multiple distilleries, it may be called blended Empire Rye.

Right: Stills, Van Brunt Distillery, Brooklyn, New York.

NEW YORK CITY

King's County Distillery

Brooklyn, NY 40° 41' 58.8" N, 73° 58' 48.7" W

When Colin Spoelman and David Haskell founded Kings County Distillery in 2010, it was the first distillery to make whiskey in Brooklyn, New York, since Prohibition. Despite Spoelman's Kentucky roots, Kings County decided to take a different approach to making bourbon. They started with a two-grain mash bill consisting of 80% New York-grown organic corn and 20% malted barley, which allowed them to sell it unaged as corn whiskey and let it rest in charred new oak barrels to make bourbon. Beyond its local grains, Kings County has also sought to add New York terroir to its whiskey by fermenting it in open-topped wooden fermenters made from the same cedar as the water tanks

Below: Scottish-made Forsyth pot stills at Kings County Distillery, Brooklyn, New York.

that dot the New York skyline. The wash is double distilled in Scottish pot stills and then aged. At the beginning, Kings County aged its whiskey in small barrels, but it has since gradually sized up. Similarly, Kings County whiskeys were only available in 375ml hip-flask bottles until 2020 when they launched a custom full-sized 750ml bottle that still matches their style. In 2016, the American Distilling Institute named Kings County Distillery its Distillery of the Year due to its high standards, leadership and camaraderie in the craft spirits industry.

WHISKEYS

MASH BILL: 80% NEW YORK-GROWN DANKO RYE, 20% ENGLISH MALTED BARLEY

Kings County Distillery Empire Rye Straight Rye Whiskey
51% ABV (102 proof)

IF YOU TRY ONE...

Kings County Distillery Empire Rye Straight Rye Whiskey 51% ABV (102 proof)

At first smell, there are lovely aromas of caramel apple with just a touch of sweet cinnamon spice, with faint notes of rye bread and liquorice underneath. On the palate, it is delicious and full with wonderfully integrated flavours of rye, baking spice, baked apple and vanilla, and good oak structure to balance the sweeter elements. The finish is long and has sweet notes of cinnamon, nutmeg and a slight sugar glaze. This is a fantastic whiskey that at 51% ABV is not harsh and shows depth of character even at two years old. Kings County continues to illustrate its great whiskey-making skills, and if you are a fan of rye, this is a must-buy. Enjoy however you like, but it is excellent neat, though if you find the alcohol a bit strong, try a little splash of water, and it makes a fantastic New York Sour (see page 182).

Above: Kings County Distillery Empire Rye Straight Rye Whiskey.

Van Brunt Stillhouse

Brooklyn, NY 40° 40' 24.6" N, 74° 00' 36.4" W

Daric Schlesselman and his wife Sarah Ludington founded Van Brunt Stillhouse in 2012, and began by making a few spirits including rum, grappa, moonshine and whiskey. The Van Brunt name comes from a Dutch farmer and possible distiller who lived in what became Brooklyn, New York. As with many craft distillers, Van Brunt began by ageing their spirits in small barrels to speed up maturation, though over time they have transitioned to using more medium and full-sized barrels. Both their corn and rye are grown in New York. Van Brunt was also an early adopter of Empire Rye. Theirs is distilled from a two-grain mash of New York rye and malted barley, and makes a great spirit.

WHISKEYS

MASH BILL: 75% DANKO RYE, 25% MALTED BARLEY

Van Brunt Stillhouse Empire Rye Whiskey 42% ABV (84 proof)

Above: Van Brunt Stillhouse Empire Rye Whiskey.

IF YOU TRY ONE...

Van Brunt Stillhouse Empire Rye Whiskey

42% ABV (84 proof)

A lovely aroma of rye grain, baking spice, malty biscuit notes, sweet cherries and a hint of black liquorice and oak. The palate is well balanced with sweet barrel notes of dried cherries paired with typical spicy rye flavours and oak. On the finish, there are lingering flavours of oak, cherries, brown sugar and just a touch of black tea. This is one of the best whiskeys ever produced by Van Brunt. It has good fruit sweetness combined with rye spice and oak that is in excellent balance. At 42% ABV, it is soft enough to enjoy neat, but it is also ideal for a Manhattan cocktail.

HUDSON VALLEY

Coppersea Distilling

New Paltz, NY 41° 46' 43.1" N, 74° 05' 23.7" W

Michael Kinstlick and Angus MacDonald founded Coppersea Distilling in 2012 with the vision of creating whiskeys as they were in the 18th and 19th centuries before industrialization. MacDonald and distiller

Above: Coppersea Distilling, New Paltz, New York.

Christopher Williams developed a system of floor malting their own grain (see photograph, page 173), which in the 21st century was an almost completely lost art. Their first spirits included an unaged whiskey called Raw Rye and a few eaux-de-vie made from various local fruits. Coppersea work with local farmers to grow their grains, and even buy their barrels from a cooper that makes them from New York oak in a move Williams described as obnoxiously authentic, but with the sole intent of creating great spirits that are the truest expression of the Hudson Valley and New York that they can make. Take a sip of their whiskey and all that work shines through.

WHISKEYS

MASH BILL: 100% HUDSON VALLEY FLOOR-MALTED RYE

Coppersea Bonticou Crag Straight Rye Malt Whisky 48% ABV (96 proof)

– **Bottled in Bond** 50% ABV (100 proof)

MASH BILL: 80% RYE, 20% MALTED BARLEY

Excelsior Straight Rye Whisky 48% ABV (96 proof)

Above: Bonticou Crag Bottled in Bond Straight Rye Malt Whisky.

IF YOU TRY ONE...

Bonticou Crag Bottled in Bond Straight Rye Malt Whisky 50% ABV (100 proof)

The nose is jam-packed full of aromas of stone fruit, caramel brittle, vanilla, live oak and fresh cut grass. On the palate, there are flavours of fennel, salted caramel, vanilla, sweet cherries, dried pineapple, peaches and cream, maple and sassafras, followed by a pronounced dryness from the oak tannins. And while the finish is bone dry, simultaneously there are rich flavours of raisins, dried cherries, maple syrup, vanilla, hazelnuts and a sweet oloroso sherry, with just a hint of grassiness from the malted rye. Bonticou Crag is a beautiful voyage of flavour that interweaves elements of wood, fennel, rye spice and complex sweetness. This fantastic whiskey is deserving of being sipped neat or opened with just a splash of water. If you are a fan of complex whiskeys that are sweet, woody and spicy, it is a must.

Tuthilltown Spirits

Gardiner, NY 41° 41' 10.9" N, 74° 10' 36.1" W

Ralph Erenzo and Brian Lee founded Tuthilltown Spirits in 2003 when their first idea of creating a retreat for rock climbers hit a roadblock. When they opened, Tuthilltown was the first New York whiskey distiller since the end of Prohibition. In 2010, Tuthilltown Spirits was named Distillery of the Year by the American Distilling Institute, and in April 2017, the company was fully purchased by William Grant & Sons, the third-largest producer of Scotch whisky in the UK.

WHISKEYS

MASH BILL: 95% RYE, 5% MALTED BARLEY

Hudson Do The Rye Thing New York Straight Rye Whiskey 46% ABV (92 proof)

IF YOU TRY ONE...

Hudson Do The Rye Thing New York Straight Rye Whiskey 46% ABV (92 proof)

On the nose, there are notes of chocolate, rye bread, grape jelly, oak and white wine. It is big and chewy on the palate, with flavours of rye bread, caramel, seasoned oak and just a touch of grassiness from the locally grown rye. The finish is as smooth as silk and tastes of rye bread with just a touch of honey. This is a really delicious whiskey that illustrates that there is so much good whiskey to drink in the world if you give young distilleries time and money to develop from interesting to great.

Above: Hudson Do The Rye Thing New York Straight Rye Whiskey.

WESTERN NEW YORK

Five & 20 Spirits

Westfield, NY 42° 18' 34.5" N, 79° 36' 19.1" W

The Mazza family, who founded Five & 20 Spirits in 2005, emigrated from Italy in the mid-1950s and settled in North East, Pennsylvania on the shore of Lake Erie.

In his homeland, patriarch Joseph Mazza had worked 40 acres (16 hectares) of orchard and vineyards, so creating a winery in America came naturally to him. When the law changed and New York drastically reduced the cost of opening a distillery (see page 171), the Mazzas decided to expand their business, setting up a second winery and a small distillery in Mayville, New York, just 20 miles (32km) away from their home in Pennsylvania. In 2013, the NY winery and distillery moved to an 80-acre (32.4-hectare) farm in Westfield, where they now make whiskey, brandy and liqueurs.

WHISKEYS

MASH BILL: 80% RYE, 20% MALTED BARLEY

Five & 20 Spirits Straight Rye Whiskey 45% ABV (90 proof)

Five & 20 Spirits Rye Whiskey
– **Finished in Port Casks** 49.5% ABV (99 proof)
– **Finished in Sherry Casks** 49.5% ABV (99 proof)

Above: Five & 20 Spirits Straight Rye Whiskey.

IF YOU TRY ONE...

Five & 20 Spirits Straight Rye Whiskey

45% ABV (90 proof)

The nose is somewhat closed, but there are some green barrel notes mixed with caramel and a touch of rye spice. On the tongue, it is very sweet, full of caramel and brown sugar, with a touch of young oak and rye. As you continue to sip, there are more baking spice notes, though the two central flavour types remain. On the finish, the sweet flavours fade away and the core flavours of rye and wood shine through with a lingering note of green corn husk. This is a well-distilled whiskey but it's possible that, if the barrel staves were seasoned longer, it would allow more complex flavours to develop.

Myer Farm Distillers

Ovid, NY 42° 40' 09.1" N, 76° 43' 57.2" W

Brothers Joe and John Myer, who founded Myer Farm Distillers in 2012, are descended from Andrew Dunlap and Joseph Wilson, two of the first settlers in Ovid, New York. The Myer family purchased their first farm in 1810 and moved to their current farm in 1868. John runs the family farm growing corn and soya beans, winter and spring wheat, triticale, spelt, barley, rye, oats, clover and alfalfa. Joe, an experienced dairyman, is now their head distiller and all their spirits production uses just 10 per cent of the total grain yield from the farm. The distillery makes vodka, gin, whiskey and liqueurs, and almost all their spirits have won multiple awards, with their Cayuga Gold Barrel-Aged Gin being consistently voted one of the best in the nation. For their rye whiskey, they distil a mash of 70% rye, with the other 30% consisting of corn and malted barley. Technically, their rye whiskey has 5% less rye grain than the standard for Empire Rye, but given their process, it is definitely a strong example of New York rye whiskey.

WHISKEYS

MASH BILL: 70% RYE, 30% CORN, MALTED BARLEY

John Myer New York Straight Rye Whiskey
– **Original** 45% ABV (90 proof)
– **Single Barrel** 45% ABV (90 proof)

IF YOU TRY ONE...

John Myer New York Straight Rye Whiskey
45% ABV (90 proof)

Apples galore! On the nose, there are aromas of baked apple, cinnamon and nutmeg, while on the palate, it tastes of baked apple and spices, with a warm touch of vanilla and wood to round things out. The finish is slightly warm with lingering flavours of baked apple and pear, followed by some usual rye spice notes and just a touch of oak. A very tasty whiskey full of light fruit flavour and warm spice.

Above: John Myer New York Straight Rye Whiskey.

The New York Sour as we know it today was first made in Chicago in the 1880s as a variant of the classic Whiskey Sour. The original recipe, known as the Continental Sour, called for a float of claret, a British term for red wine from Bordeaux. The New York Sour has been known by a few names and broadly refers to a Whiskey Sour made with a red wine float, with the option to use rye or bourbon and egg white or not. However, for both historical and flavour reasons, it is reasonable to argue that a standard New York Sour starts with rye, though other whiskeys are acceptable variants of the drink. A dry red wine will make the overall drink very dry, so if you would prefer the drink to be a bit sweeter, consider using a less dry wine or port.

New York Sour

MAKES 1

60ml (2fl oz) **rye whiskey**

30ml (1fl oz) **lemon juice**

22ml (¾fl oz) **simple syrup**

15ml (½fl oz) **red wine**

1 **egg white** (optional)

Fill a cocktail shaker with ice, add the rye whiskey, lemon juice and simple syrup and shake. Strain into an Old-Fashioned glass with fresh ice. Slowly pour the red wine over the back of a (bar) spoon to float the wine on top of the drink.

Egg white variation: Add all the ingredients including the egg white but not the red wine to a cocktail shaker. Shake without ice for about 30 seconds. Open the shaker, add ice and shake a second time until cold. Strain into an Old-Fashioned glass with fresh ice. Slowly pour the red wine over the back of a (bar) spoon to float the wine on top of the drink.

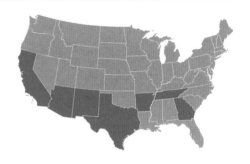

Southern states
Smoked whiskey

Legally, American smoked whiskeys can be made in any state, but there is an interesting concentration of them in the southern part of the United States. While some distillers in the region have chosen to use peat to flavour their whiskeys, a good number of others use woods such as apple, cherry, hickory and mesquite to smoke their grains, among the latter camp those drawing inspiration from the flavours of southern and southwestern barbecue. American smoked whiskey is a relatively young category and yet some of those made in the southern United States have set a high bar for quality while displaying a distinctive regional character.

History

The creation of smoked whiskeys is largely a historical consequence of converting raw barley into malt. At its root, malting is the controlled process by which humans can prepare grain to convert its internal starch into fermentable sugars for making beer or whiskey. Raw

Opposite: The Colorado River winding its way through the Grand Canyon near Page, Arizona.

Climatic conditions: Atlanta, GA – 8 active distilleries

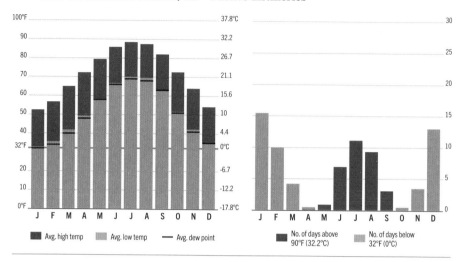

barley is soaked in water, which cues the dormant seed to begin the germination process to grow a new plant. However, once the seeds' internal enzymes have been fully activated, the grain is re-dried in a kiln, which holds the malt in stasis until a brewer or distiller is ready to use it. It is during this last step of kiln drying that malt can pick up smoke flavours.

Traditional kilns were large spaces with floors made of perforated materials such as tile, brick or iron that would allow smoke and hot air to rise from the furnace below and dry out the malt. And what material was burned in

Region Name:	Georgia, Tennessee, Arkansas, Texas, New Mexico, Arizona, Southern California
Nickname:	Various
Capital Cities:	Atlanta, Nashville, Little Rock, Austin, Santa Fe, Phoenix, Los Angeles
Population:	82,696,621
Number of Active Distilleries:	363
Whiskey Fact:	Smoked whiskeys are usually made with malted barley because it is both a common whiskey grain and one of the best at absorbing smoke flavours.

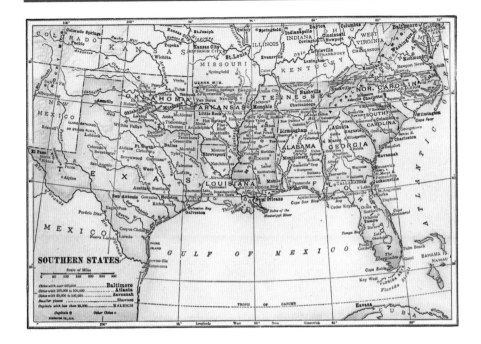

the furnace would dictate the type and intensity of the smoke flavour left on the grain. In Britain, malt destined for brewers would have been dried with mild materials such as hay, beech wood or anthracite so that the resulting beer did not have a strong malt flavour. However, in Scotland, malt destined for whiskey was kiln dried with peat fires, as it was cheap, was widely available and added a pleasant flavour to the whiskey once it was distilled and rested in a barrel.

In contrast, most American whiskey, both during the early Republic and today, is made with raw grains that are not malted and never encounter smoke. As mentioned in previous chapters, most American whiskey, be it bourbon or rye, is made from a mash of grains that usually contains only a small amount of malted barley for its enzymes necessary for fermentation. And since most early American malt would have been destined for beer, it is likely that maltsters would have used neutral woods or other combustible materials that would not have imparted a strong smoke flavour. As a result, it is reasonable to assume that early American whiskey had little smoky

Above: An official map of the southern states, drawn in 1898.

Climatic conditions: Santa Fe, NM – 5 active distilleries

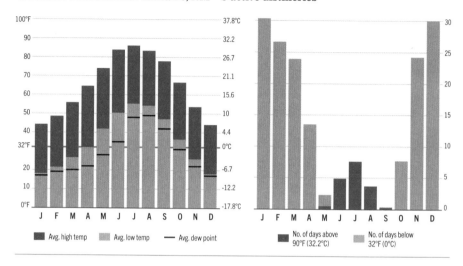

Avg. high temp   Avg. low temp   — Avg. dew point   No. of days above 90°F (32.2°C)   No. of days below 32°F (0°C)

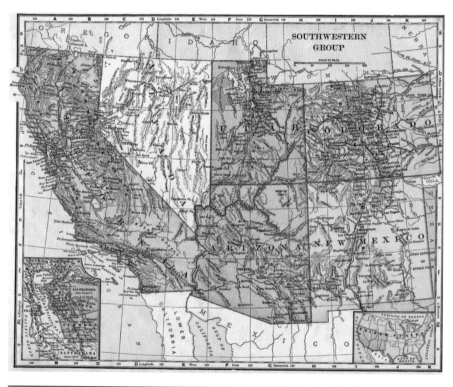

flavour. And what smoke character there might have been in the 18th century would have quickly disappeared in the 19th century as maltsters developed technologies to kiln dry malt with indirect air that contained no smoke.

However, in the modern era of craft distillers, people have begun to experiment with smoke and look to distilling traditions outside of the United States for inspiration. One of the earliest examples came from an Oregon distiller whose passion for single malt Scotch whisky inspired him to make his own peated malt whiskey (see page 209). Not long after, American smoked whiskeys divided roughly into two groups: those that used peated malt, and those that used other novel sources of smoke inspired by local resources and culinary traditions, with many of the latter located in the lower half of the country stretching from Georgia to Southern California. For today's fan of smoke flavours, be it in cheese, meat, fish, beer, Scotch or mezcal,

Opposite: An official map of the southwestern states, drawn in 1896.

Left: A British maltman tending to a peat-burning furnace circa 1940. The peat would send up a stream of fragrant smoke to the loft where the barley was dried.

Like the country itself, American barbecue is the result of the multicultural exchange that took place between Indigenous peoples, African slaves and European settlers. At its core, traditional barbecue is the process of slow-cooking meat over a wood fire for as many as 24 hours. Wood flavours are absorbed into the meat and mingle with the spices and sauces that vary widely from state to state and even county to county. It is commonly accepted that the word 'barbecue' comes from the Taíno language of the Caribbean that the Spanish transliterated as *barbacoa*. The Taíno had a practice of roasting food over coals, set on a wooden frame. By the 18th century, barbecue was fully entrenched in the American culture, and George Washington recorded attending and hosting six barbecues, one of which – on 27 May 1769 – he describes as lasting well into the night. With these deep roots in the culture and palate of Americans, it is no real surprise that woods such as oak, hickory, apple, mesquite and others common in barbecue would find their way into American whiskey.

Southern smoked whiskeys are a good starting point to explore the category and experience smoke-flavoured whiskeys in a uniquely American context.

Production requirements

There are no legal standards in the United States specifically for smoked whiskey. Because of this, any whiskey that meets the Standards of Identity for its class and type (bourbon, rye, wheat, corn whiskey and so on)

can use smoked grains to add flavour to the spirit. While one could potentially percolate smoke through a spirit to add flavour, the near universally accepted method is to mash, ferment and distil smoked grains to introduce the desired flavour. By using this method, distillers can control the intensity of the smoke flavour in a whiskey by varying how heavily the grains are smoked and what proportion they make up of the mash bill. Similar to smoking meats, how much smoke flavour is absorbed by the grain can depend on its temperature and how moist the grain is. In general, smoke sticks better to colder as opposed to warmer surfaces, and wetter as opposed to drier surfaces. In addition, grains smoked for longer periods of time will absorb more flavour than those with shorter exposure to smoke, which is why barley is usually smoked during the malting process. And one benefit of using smoked grains to make whiskey is that, when done correctly, it can hide some of the rough edges of a young whiskey and make it taste more mature than its numerical age would suggest.

Above: Veronica Townsend, head distiller and maltster drying malt with mesquite smoke at Hamilton Distillers, Tucson, Arizona.

SOUTHERN SMOKED WHISKEY
distilleries to try

MIDDLE TENNESSEE

Corsair Distillery

Nashville, TN 36 °09' 54.3" N, 86° 47' 42.4" W

Darek Bell and Andrew Webber founded Corsair in 2008 after exploring the idea of building a bio-diesel plant and realizing that making whiskey would be more interesting. While many craft distillers have spun complicated tales about their distilling heritage, Corsair has proudly represented itself as a modern distillery. They have looked to push boundaries and helped to create entirely new categories of American whiskey like smoked and hopped whiskeys. Their first distillery was in Bowling Green, Kentucky, and two years later they opened a second distillery in Nashville, Tennessee and began to rack up 800 medals from various competitions. In 2012, the American Distilling Institute (ADI) named their Grainiac 9 Grain Bourbon the Best American Whiskey, and in 2013, *Whiskey Advocate* awarded their Triple Smoke Artisan Whiskey of the Year. With all this experimentation, Corsair was also extremely open, publishing two books with specific information about what did and did not work and how other craft distillers could smoke and malt their own grains. Because of their leadership in the industry and quality spirits, the ADI named Corsair their 2014 Distillery of the Year.

Above: Corsair Triple Smoke American Single Malt Whiskey.

WHISKEYS
MASH BILL: 100% MALTED BARLEY

Corsair Triple Smoke American Single Malt Whiskey 40% ABV (80 proof) Made with cherry, beechwood and peat smoked barley.

Corsair Hydra American Single Malt Whiskey 42% ABV (84 proof) This was distilled from malt smoked with pecan, apple, sugar maple, black walnut and persimmon woods, but discontinued in 2019.

Corsair Triple Smoke American Single Malt Whiskey

40% ABV (80 proof)

The nose is really nice with an interesting combination of peat, sweet cherries and malty biscuits. On the palate, the whiskey starts sweet and then opens with more bright notes of candied citrus, malt and light peat smoke. On the finish, the peat intensifies, though rather than becoming a total smoke bomb it is moderated by beechwood, giving the flavour a light lift at the end and leaving the palate with soft lingering notes of fresh cherries and homemade lemonade. Triple Smoke is an incredibly complex whiskey given that it is only a year old. The smoke does not cover up youthful whiskey so much as allow it to evolve a more mature flavour in a shorter period. If the idea of peated whiskey with notes of cherry interests you, this will do an excellent job of scratching that itch. And at 45% ABV, it can easily be drunk neat, with a splash of water or in any cocktail that calls for Scotch.

Above: Stills at Corsair Distillery, Nashville, Tennessee.

Balcones Distilling

Waco, TX 31° 33' 01.6" N, 97° 08' 08.3" W

Founded in 2008, Balcones is known for being an innovative distillery (see page 93). One of their early innovations was taking their Baby Blue Corn Whisky and smoking it with Texas scrub oak using a 'secret' process. While there is no definitive answer to what this process is exactly, it is possible that the whiskey is placed in a tank and then the smoke percolated through the liquid, resulting in two spirits with only one fermentation, distillation and ageing regimen. Balcones also makes a few expressions of American single malt whiskey, which might sound like an odd choice in an area with such a hot climate, but they have worked out well. One of these was distilled from 100% peated malt imported from Scotland and aged in charred new oak barrels in Waco, Texas.

Below: The warehouse at Balcones Distilling, Waco, Texas.

WHISKEYS

MASH BILL: 100% HOPI BLUE CORN

Balcones Brimstone Texas Scrub Oak Smoked Whisky 53% ABV
(106 proof)

MASH BILL: 100% MALTED BARLEY

Balcones Peated Texas Single Malt Whisky 63% ABV (126 proof)

IF YOU TRY ONE...
Balcones Brimstone Texas Scrub
Oak Smoked Whisky 53% ABV (106 proof)

The nose is dense and sweet, with notes of molasses and
sarsaparilla paired with Texas smoked brisket and corn
bread. On the palate, it is hot, though not surprisingly
for 53% ABV. The spirit has a nice sweet and smoky
character, a bit like artisan root beer and barbecue.
The smoke is quite reserved with more of the grain and
barrel coming through. The finish has long sweet and
smoky flavours that linger in your mouth reminiscent of
eating brisket burnt ends. If you like barbecue, drinking
Brimstone is a must. It captures Texas barbecue in the
glass and immerses you in the tastes and smells of the
world's best pit-house.

*Above: Balcones Brimstone Texas
Scrub Oak Smoked Whisky.*

SONORAN DESERT

Hamilton Distillers

Tucson, Arizona 32° 14' 53.1" N, 110° 59' 33.5" W

Stephen Paul and his daughter Amanda founded
Hamilton Distillers in 2011. Five years earlier, Paul was
sipping Scotch and barbecuing when he was struck
with the idea to use mesquite to smoke malted barley
and capture the essence of the Sonoran Desert. Looking
to root his spirits in their place, Paul chose the name
Whiskey Del Bac, which refers to a local mission and
translates as 'of the place where the river reappears in
the sand'. While Paul continued to work as a custom
furniture maker, he studied the process of malting
barley and making whiskey, and in 2013, he released

three expressions of American single malt whiskey: unaged Old Pueblo, unsmoked malt Classic and mesquite smoked American single malt Dorado.

WHISKEYS

MASH BILL: 100% MALTED BARLEY

Whiskey Del Bac Dorado American Single Malt Whiskey
45% ABV (90 proof)

Whiskey Del Bac American Single Malt Whiskey Distiller's Cut Fall 2020 Cask Strength ABV varies A blend of Whiskey Del Bac Dorado and Classic Sonoran single malts finished in select barrels.

IF YOU TRY ONE...

Whiskey Del Bac Dorado American Single Malt Whiskey 45% ABV (90 proof)

The combination of malt and mesquite smoke is captivating and combines notes of fresh plum and malt reminiscent of British scones with clotted cream and jam. On the palate, the malt and mesquite flavours are more robust and include notes of stone fruit, vanilla and just a touch of toffee. On the finish, it warms the mouth and the smoke flavour grows bolder into a mesquite campfire, with a touch of honeyed malt. With a pronounced smoke flavour, Dorado is more in line with a Scotch of medium peat intensity while still retaining an incredibly good underlying malt character. It is an excellent whiskey.

Above: Whiskey Del Bac Dorado American Single Malt Whiskey.

SOUTHERN CALIFORNIA

Stark Spirits

Pasadena CA, 34° 10' 07.0" N, 118° 09' 31.4" W

Greg Stark and his wife Karen Robinson-Stark founded Stark Spirits in 2013. While working a full career in information technology, Greg pursued his passion for making mead and home brewing, but in the early 2000s it was time for a change. Stark looked seriously at building a hydroponic fish farm to raise tuna, but in the end craft distilling won out, being a creative outlet for both him and Karen. Stark went to work laying down barrels of whiskey while he made rum and distilled a one-of-a-kind brandy from locally grown Valencia oranges and Karen developed a couple of expressions of gin. In 2016, Stark Spirits released their California Single Malt Whiskey, distilled from unpeated malt and aged in a combination of new oak and used bourbon barrels, and in addition a peated single malt, distilled from imported Scottish peated malt. In 2017, Stark Spirits' Peated Single Malt Whiskey earned a Double Gold medal and was name the best American Smoked Whiskey at the American Distilling Institute's Judging of Craft Spirits.

WHISKEYS

MASH BILL: 100% MALTED BARLEY

Spark Spirits Peated Single Malt Whiskey 46% ABV (92 proof)
– Cask Strength ABV varies

IF YOU TRY ONE...
Spark Spirits Peated Single Malt Whiskey
46% ABV (92 proof)

The nose is surprisingly light and bright for a peated malt. The peat is definitely there, but it is more of an accent than the star of the show. In addition, there are also lovely notes of honey, heather and sweet orange. On the palate, it warms the tongue and has more peat flavour that is balanced with honey, golden raspberries and an excellent malt whiskey base. The smoke continues to grow on the finish, though it is still not overpowering. There is a pleasant malt chocolate flavour combined with lemon leaf and oak. This is a lovely whiskey that shows great restraint with the peat, allowing it to complement rather than dominate the malt flavour.

Above: Spark Spirits Peated Single Malt Whiskey.

First created by Kyle Jamieson at Edinburgh's Panda &
Sons, Smokin' Word is a variation of the pre-Prohibition
classic Last Word. While the original cocktail combined
equal parts gin, Chartreuse, maraschino and lime juice,
this modern take substitutes peated whiskey for the gin
and lemon juice for the lime juice. Even though Smokin'
Word was created in Scotland, it is a great cocktail to
highlight the character of American smoked whiskeys.

Smokin' Word

MAKES 1

30ml (1fl oz) **smoked whiskey**

15ml (½fl oz) **Yellow Chartreuse**

15ml (½fl oz) **maraschino liqueur**

15ml (½fl oz) **lemon juice**

maraschino cherry, to garnish

Combine all the ingredients in a cocktail
shaker filled with ice. Shake, then strain
into a chilled cocktail glass. Garnish with
a maraschino cherry.

Pacific Northwest
American single malt whiskey

The Pacific Northwest is a great region for making American single malt whiskey. Unlike bourbon and rye that can stand up well to hot temperatures in new oak, single malt whiskey can become overwhelmed. However, the Pacific Northwest is known for its more moderate temperatures and frequent rainfall due to its position on the Pacific Ocean. In addition, the region has long been at or near the top of the nation's barley production. So, with moderate temperatures, tons of barley and clean mountain water, it is no surprise that the Pacific Northwest is producing some of the best American single malts in the country.

History

Between the 1830s and 1870, it is estimated that some 400,000 immigrants made their way west along the Oregon Trail. For many of them, their journey began in Independence, Missouri, travelling overland through Nebraska and Wyoming before snaking their way

Opposite: Mount Hood, the highest mountain in Oregon and the fourth highest peak in the Cascade Range.

Climatic conditions: Portland, OR – 17 active distilleries

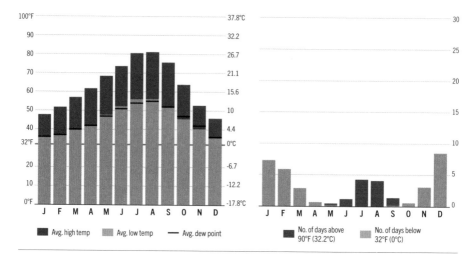

Legend (left chart): Avg. high temp · Avg. low temp · Avg. dew point

Legend (right chart): No. of days above 90°F (32.2°C) · No. of days below 32°F (0°C)

through the Rocky Mountains into southern Idaho and western Oregon. After arriving in Oregon's Willamette Valley, many settlers would head either north into Washington or south further into Oregon. A lot of these settlers were homesteaders who cleared land and began farming and raising livestock. However, some of them became merchants.

As in Missouri, some of the most successful liquor merchants in the Pacific Northwest were recent immigrants who imported and sold bourbon and rye whiskeys from Kentucky and other eastern states. Men such as William Shepperd Norman from

Above: The Pride of Oregon Old Bourbon advertisement, 1871.

Region Name:	States of Oregon, Washington, Idaho
Nickname:	The Beaver State, the Evergreen State, the Gem State
Capital Cities:	Salem, Olympia, Boise
Population:	13,619,695
Number of Active Distilleries:	204
Whiskey Fact:	Since 2011, Washington State University has had its own Bread Lab where new regional varieties of grain are developed for wholegrain milling, baking, cooking, malting, brewing and distilling into whiskey.

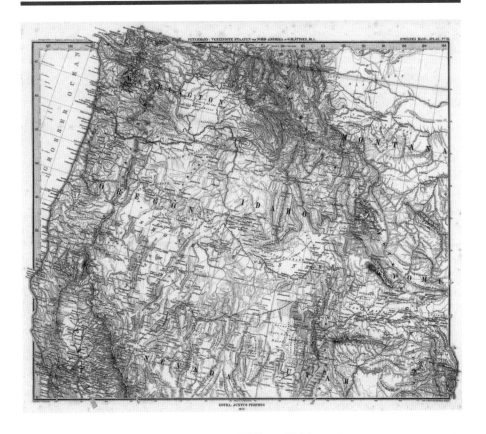

England, Lazard Coblentz from France, William Fahle and Solomon Blumauer of Germany and Giuseppe, Francesco Giovanni and Stephano Angelo Arata from Italy all built successful liquor businesses. But each was undone as Washington, Oregon and Idaho passed their own statewide prohibition laws in 1914, 1916 and 1917 respectively. After the repeal of National Prohibition in 1933, each of these states set up their own systems to control the distribution and sale of alcohol.

Shortly after Repeal, only a couple of distilleries opened in the region and focused their production on brandy, bourbon, blended whiskey, gin, vodka and liqueurs, but no single malt. The first American single malt whiskey to be distilled and aged in the Pacific Northwest was McCarthy's Oregon Single Malt Whiskey

Above: An official map of the Pacific Northwest, printed in 1875.

(see page 210), which was distilled in 1996 and first released in 1999. A decade later, craft distillers were proliferating throughout the region and several had begun distilling and ageing their own single malt whiskeys. Today, the Pacific Northwest is not alone in making American single malt, but given its climate and abundance of local barley, it is likely to remain a leader in the category.

Production requirements

At the time of writing, there is no legal definition for American single malt whiskey (ASMW), so consequently there is no legal description for Pacific Northwest ASMW. In the current Standards of Identity, malt whiskey is defined as a whiskey distilled to not more than 160 proof (80% ABV) from a fermented mash of not less than 51% malted barley, stored at not more than 125 proof (62.5% ABV) in charred new oak barrels and bottled at not less than 80 proof (40% ABV). However, by allowing US malt whiskey to contain less than 100% malted barley, this definition conflicts with most other countries that make single malt. By and large, most of the world has adopted the Scottish definition of single malt in that it is the product of one distillery (single) and distilled from a mash of 100% malted barley.

So, in 2016, nine US distilleries joined together to create the American Single Malt Whiskey Commission, with the purpose of creating an industry-accepted definition for ASMW, and to have that definition included in the Federal Standards of Identity. The first task was fairly straightforward. The founding members constructed the standard for ASMW in such a way that they believed it would give distillers the widest range of production practices while still being recognizable to consumers as corollaries to single malts made in other countries, and without presenting significant regulatory challenges for the Alcohol and Tobacco Tax and Trade Bureau (TTB). In the end they settled on the following six-part definition: ASMW must be made from 100% malted barley; distilled entirely at one distillery; mashed, distilled and matured in the United States; matured

Above: Barley growing in a field.

in oak casks not exceeding 700 litres (185 US gallons); distilled to no more than 160 proof (80% ABV); bottled at 80 proof (40% ABV) or more. Since its foundation, the commission has now signed up 170 member distilleries.

Then in 2019, TTB opened a public comment period stating that they were considering several technical and structural changes to the alcohol regulation that would better reflect industry practices and help improve the label approval process. The American Single Malt Whiskey Commission, distillers and a few other industry associations provided feedback to TTB on their proposals and took the opportunity to request that a standard for ASMW be added to the regulations. TTB issued a final ruling early in 2020 addressing some of the feedback they had received and stating that other aspects would be addressed at a future date. So, while ASMW has no legal definition, distillers are united in what they believe it should mean and how they plan to make their whiskeys.

Above: Westland Distillery mash house, Seattle, Washington.

OREGON COAST

Rogue Ales & Spirits

Newport, OR 44° 37' 14.4" N, 124° 02' 53.1" W

Jack Joyce, Rob Strasser and Bob Woodell founded Rogue Ales in Ashland, Oregon in 1988, and a year later they began construction of a new brewpub in Newport on the Oregon coast, with John Maier coming in as head brewer. Fast-forward to 2003, and Rogue Ales were operating several brewpubs including one in Portland's Pearl District. This site became the first home of Rogue Spirits, where they started making rum. Around 2008 or 2009, Rogue built its second distillery out in Newport where they began to make vodka, whiskey, gin and a few other spirits. In 2013, Rogue released their first bottles of Dead Guy Whiskey, which at that time was only aged for one month before being bottled. Two years later, Rogue

Below: Dead Guy Whiskey bottles on display, Rogue Ales & Spirits, Newport, Oregon.

opened their own cooperage called Rolling Thunder Barrel Works, making Rogue one of an exceedingly small handful of distilleries that make their own barrels. Today, Rogue make a rye malt whiskey and four American single malts including Dead Guy Whiskey, which is now bottled from whiskeys that have aged for at least two years before they are vatted, proofed and bottled.

WHISKEYS

MASH BILL: 100% MALTED BARLEY

Rogue Spirits Dead Guy Whiskey 40% ABV (80 proof) Made with grains as for Dead Guy Ale: two-row malted barley, crystal malt and Munich malt.

Rogue Spirits Oregon Single Malt Whiskey 40% ABV (80 proof)

Rogue Spirits Rolling Thunder Stouted Whiskey ABV varies

Rogue Spirits Morimoto Single Malt Whiskey 42.5% ABV (85 proof)

Above: *Rogue Spirits Dead Guy Whiskey.*

IF YOU TRY ONE...

Rogue Spirits Dead Guy Whiskey 40% ABV (80 proof)

A rich and fruity nose with notes of fresh cherries, white peach and ruby port, followed by a hint of grain and a minutely resinous character. On the palate, the sweet fruit character continues with sweet cherries and milk chocolate, which transitions on the finish to a combination of dark chocolate, candied orange peel, a resinous hop character without the bitterness and a slight tingle from the alcohol. Dead Guy is a light and fruity single malt with a somewhat resinous quality that is common among American single malts. For those interested in exploring the category, this is an excellent starting point.

PORTLAND

Bull Run Distillery

Portland, OR 45° 32' 00.8" N, 122° 41' 53.1" W

Lee Medoff founded Bull Run Distillery in 2010 with the goal of making pure Oregon single malt whiskey. Unlike other craft distillers, Bull Run was not Medoff's first introduction into the business, having begun his career as a brewer at McMenamins where he also worked as a winemaker and eventually as a distiller. Then in 2004, Medoff and his former McMenamins colleague Christian Krogstad founded House Spirits. Six years later, House's business had become largely concerned with making Aviation Gin, which was a huge success, before being sold in 2016. Wanting to focus more on aged spirits, Medoff created Bull Run, which sold vodka and sourced whiskey and rum while its own single malt aged. Bull Run partnered with Burnside Brewing to make their 100% barley mash, which Medoff purposefully ferments hot with ale yeast to produce a lot of fruity esters. After distillation, the new make is then aged in charred new oak casks until it is ready.

WHISKEYS

MASH BILL: 100% MALTED BARLEY

Bull Run Oregon Single Malt Whiskey Aged 6 Years 45.18% ABV (90.36 proof)

Bull Run Oregon Single Malt Whiskey Finished in Oregon Pinot Noir Casks 52.55% ABV (105.1 proof)

IF YOU TRY ONE...

Bull Run Oregon Single Malt Whiskey Aged 6 Years
45.18% ABV (90.36 proof)

The nose has an agreeable and strong aroma of malted chocolate and roasted peanuts, layered with nice wood notes. As the whiskey opens, softer fruit notes begin to shine through. On the palate, it is soft and nutty, with a resinous wood character layered with milk chocolate and a hint of menthol. The finish is soft and medium long, with a slight nuttiness followed by strong terpene flavours like you would find in hops or cannabis. This single malt has a lot of pleasant flavours traditionally found in malt whiskey, though it seems the use of all new charred oak barrels causes the softer malt character to pick up some resinous or cannabinoid flavours that give it a distinct earthy character strongly associated with the Pacific Northwest.

Above: Bull Run Oregon Single Malt Whiskey Aged 6 Years.

Clear Creek Distillery

Hood River, OR 45° 42' 47.7" N, 121° 31' 03.4" W

Steve McCarthy founded Clear Creek Distillery in 1985 to create world-renowned fruit brandies from the abundance of the Pacific Northwest's best orchards. As the story goes, McCarthy, whose family had grown pears and apples in Mount Hood for four generations, discovered European fruit brandies while travelling to Europe for work, which sparked him on his return to create an eau-de-vie from Bartlett pears grown in his family's orchards. About a decade later, McCarthy's love of peated Scotch inspired him to make his own expression in Oregon. Since Clear Creek was not set up to mash grain, McCarthy had a local brewery mash and lauter (filter) the 100% peated malt that he imported from Scotland. Clear Creek then fermented and distilled the whiskey in a single pass using a Holstein pot still, and aged it for three years in barrels made from air-dried Oregon oak. In 2014, Hood River

Distillers purchased Clear Creek Distillery and moved their distilling operation from Portland to Hood River, though they have continued to use the same recipes and practices that McCarthy perfected over his 30-year career as a distiller.

WHISKEYS

MASH BILL: 100% MALTED BARLEY

McCarthy's Oregon Single Malt Whiskey 42.5% ABV (85 proof)

....

IF YOU TRY ONE...

McCarthy's Oregon Single Malt Whiskey

42.5% ABV (85 proof)

At first whiff, it has a lovely, captivating aroma of peated malt that is a mixture of iodine, Band-Aid plaster, orange blossoms, light honey and malt, with just a hint of chocolate. The first sip is like being transported to a bonfire on the beach next to the ocean, where brined meats are smoked with hickory. As you continue to sip, the once distinct smoke character fades into the background and you notice sweet and bready notes like American biscuits drizzled with honey. It has a long and soft finish that envelops you in warm smoked hickory flavours that seem to be a combination of peat mingling with the Oregon oak barrel. At three years old, McCarthy's is delicious, soft and well structured. It is a testament to the fact that good single malt does not need to age for decades to realize its potential but needs care and attention to find the right combination of grains and barrels.

Above: McCarthy's Oregon Single Malt Whiskey.

CENTRAL OREGON

Bendistillery

Bend, OR 44° 09' 37.9" N, 121° 21' 34.0" W

Jim Bendis founded Bendistillery in 1996 to create premium vodkas and gin shaped by the Oregon landscape. The distillery name is a play on both the name of the founder and their original location in downtown Bend.

In 2010, Bendis moved the company to a 24-acre (9.7-hectare) farm north of the city that gave them more room for distilling. One of their early whiskey experiments was to distil a batch of Deschutes Black Butte Porter and let it sit in a barrel to see what happened. Bendis was excited by the result, and in 2013, Bendistillery and Deschutes Brewery created a more formal partnership where Deschutes provides the wash without hops and Bendistillery distils and ages the whiskey in No. 4 charred new oak barrels (see page 27). The first bottling of Black Butte Malt Whiskey was three years old and released in 2016, though more recent bottlings have been made with five-year-old whiskey. Because the grain bill for Black Butte Porter includes a small amount of wheat (estimated at around 8–9%), it does not meet the standards created by the American Single Malt Whiskey Commission (see page 204), though it does qualify as malt whiskey under current US regulations.

WHISKEYS

MASH BILL: TWO-ROW MALTED BARLEY, CHOCOLATE MALT, WHEAT, CRYSTAL MALT, CARAPILS MALT

Black Butte Malt Whiskey 47% (94 proof)

IF YOU TRY ONE...

Black Butte Malt Whiskey

47% ABV (94 proof)

The aroma has an interesting mixture of bramble fruit and leaves, like eating fresh raspberries and blackberries direct from the bush in summertime, followed by a distinct note of green wood. On the palate, there is a combination of ripe plum and nectarine drizzled with honey, followed by more earthy flavours of hops, pine needles and dry timber. On the finish, the mouth warms with a pronounced resinous flavour of pine and hops mixed with a touch of vanilla and light brown sugar. Even at 47% ABV, the alcohol is not overpowering, though the flavour is quite strong, making it an excellent candidate for cocktails such as a highball, Rob Roy or the Cascadia (see page 216).

Above: Black Butte Malt Whiskey.

Orcas Island Distillery

Orcas, WA 48° 37' 20.3" N, 122° 54' 47.5" W

Charles West founded Orcas Island Distillery in 2014 with the goal of making world-class spirits from locally grown agricultural products. One fateful day, West was invited by a friend to pick apples in one of Orcas Island's heritage orchards and he decided this would be a great place for a distillery. Orcas Island once had 76,000 trees producing more than 6 million pounds (2.7 million kilograms) of heirloom apples, though demand for these older varieties has waned. West knew that these would make great brandy and he was right. His apple eau-de-vie has been named the best American apple eau-de-vie four years running at the American Distilling Institute's (ADI's) Judging of Craft Spirits. While West is not making brandy from local fruit, he is mashing, fermenting and distilling malted barley grown in Washington's Skagit Valley. The whiskey is then aged for four years and bottled at 45% ABV (90 proof). In 2019, their West Island Malt Whiskey earned a gold medal and was named the Best American Single Malt Whiskey at ADI's Judging of Craft Spirits.

WHISKEYS

MASH BILL: 100% MALTED BARLEY

Orcas Island West Island Malt Whiskey 45% ABV (90 proof)

Orcas Island West Island Malt Whiskey 45% ABV (90 proof)

The nose is a fruit bomb that starts with an intense aroma of bubblegum and transitions to notes of a fruity white wine, green apple, caramel and vanilla. On the palate, sweet notes of vanilla, caramel and nectarine cover the tongue. After swallowing, there is an intense burst of dry hops and pine that quickly fades back into sweet notes of bubblegum. This whiskey is a bit of a roller coaster of flavour that is both very fruity and resinous. This works very well in a highball or in the Cascadia cocktail (see page 216).

Above: Orcas Island West Island Malt Whiskey.

Left: Orcas Island Distillery, Orcas, Washington.

Westland Distillery

Seattle, WA 47° 34' 35.8" N, 122° 20' 03.9" W

Matt Hofmann and Emerson Lamb founded Westland
Distillery in 2010 with the singular vision of creating
a pure expression of American single malt whiskey
(ASMW) made in the Pacific Northwest. Unlike other
craft distillers who start out selling vodka and gin to
pay the bills while their whiskey ages, Westland took a
different approach. They stayed focused on ASMW and
only that. Serving as head distiller, Hofmann designed
a unique mash bill for their whiskey that consists of
Washington select pale malt, Munich malt, extra special
malt, pale chocolate malt and brown malt. Their first
few barrels were bottled in 2013 under the name Deacon
Seat, and in 2015, Westland released their core range of
American Oak, Sherry Wood and Peated American single

malts. That same year, their peated whiskey was named Best American Whiskey at the American Distilling Institute's Judging of Craft Spirits and their Sherry Wood was awarded Best Craft Whiskey by the San Francisco World Spirits Competition. The following year, it was announced that Rémy Cointreau had purchased Westland with the goal of expanding its distribution in the United States and internationally. Westland has become a leader in the movement to define ASMW and helped to found the American Single Malt Whiskey Commission (see page 204).

WHISKEYS

MASH BILL: 100% MALTED BARLEY

WESTLAND CORE RANGE:

American Oak American Single Malt Whiskey 46% ABV (92 proof)

Sherry Wood American Single Malt Whiskey 46% ABV (92 proof)

Peated American Single Malt Whiskey 46% ABV (92 proof)

Below: Westland Distillery rackhouse, Seattle, Washington.

WESTLAND OUTPOST RANGE:

Garryana American Single Malt Whiskey 50% ABV (100 proof)
A blend of malt whiskeys aged in ex-bourbon barrels and new barrels made with *Quercus garryana* (Oregon white oak).

Colere American Single Malt Whiskey 50% ABV (100 proof) Made entirely of whiskey distilled from Washington-grown Alba six-row winter barley.

Solum American Single Malt Whiskey 50% ABV (100 proof) Whiskey that is made from malted barley smoked with Washington peat.

WESTLAND LIMITED EDITION SERIES:

Distillery Exclusive Single Cask Reserve American Single Malt Whiskey ABV varies

Cask Exchange American Single Malt Whiskey ABV varies

Peat Week American Single Malt Whiskey ABV varies

Coldfoot American Single Malt 50% ABV (100 proof)

Above: *Westland Sherry Wood American Single Malt Whiskey.*

IF YOU TRY ONE...
Westland Sherry Wood American Single Malt Whiskey 46% ABV (92 proof)

The nose has a lovely aroma, with notes of marmalade, candied orange peel, roasted peanuts and marzipan, with just a touch of lemon zest, chocolate and caramel. On the palate, it is bright with a wonderful combination of malty honeyed notes and roasted peanuts, followed by a light and fruity sherry towards the tail end. The finish is bright and rich with notes of raisins, lemonade and hazelnuts. This is a beautiful whiskey that combines the core character of the American oak with layers of rich notes of dried fruit. A definite must for fans of sherried Scotch looking for an American twist.

Cascadia is an original cocktail that takes inspiration
from ingredients local to the Pacific Northwest and in
construction falls somewhere between a Rob Roy and an
Old-Fashioned. Combining Pacific Northwest American
single malt whiskey, the Italian walnut-flavoured liqueur
Nocino (making the most of the region's many walnut
trees) and honey creates an inviting herbal and spice
flavour that is perfect on cold evenings.

Cascadia

MAKES 1

60ml (2fl oz) **American single malt
whiskey**

30ml (1fl oz) **Nocino**

15ml (½fl oz) **honey syrup**

1 dash **orange bitters**

maraschino cherry or an **orange
twist** on the rim of the glass, to garnish
(optional)

Combine all the ingredients in a mixing glass
filled with ice. Stir until cold, then strain into
a chilled stemmed cocktail glass. Add the
garnish of your choice, if desired, and enjoy.

Index

Picture credits

The publishers would like to thank all the distilleries and their agents who have so kindly provided images of their bourbons and whiskeys for inclusion in this book.

Additional photographic credits are as follows:

4 Hotel Tango Distillery; **19a** Buffalo Trace Distillery; **23** Westland Distillery; **37a, 41** James E. Pepper Distillery; **43** Bluegrass Distillers. Photo Camilo Quintana; **45** James E. Pepper Distillery; **48:** Woodford Reserve; **50a** Four Roses Distillery; **53** Beam Suntory; **68** Jack Daniel's/Brown-Forman; **74** Cascade Hollow Distilling Co; **81** Nelson's Green Brier Distillery; **91, 93** Balcones Distilling; **92** Treaty Oak Distilling; **97** Milam & Greene/ Provision Spirits; **98** Treaty Oak Distilling. Photo Heather Leah Kennedy; **113** Blacksmith Distillery; **123a** Courtesy of Seagram's; **123b** MGP Ingredients; **124** Starlight Distillery. Photo Tyler Zoller; **129** Hotel Tango Distillery; **145** Painted Stave Distilling. Photo Joe del Tufo; **147b** McClintock Distilling; **154b** Beam Suntory; **155, 157** Mountain Laurel Spirits; **159** Conneaut Cellars Winery and Distillery; **162** Quantum Spirits; **172** Van Brunt Stillhouse; **173** Coppersea Distilling; **174** Kings County Distilling. Photo Valery Rizzo; **177** Coppersea Distilling; **191l & r** Whiskey Del Bac; **193l & r** Corsair Distillery; **194** Balcones Distilling; **204** Westland Distillery; **205** Westland Distillery. Photo Rafael Soldi; **206** Rogue Ales & Spirits; **212** Orcas Island. Photo Gary Speich; **213** Orcas Island Distillery; **214** Westland Distillery.

Other imagery:

1 (background) and repeats Qingwa/Can Stock Photo; **7** Addictive Stock/Stockfood; **8** Nikola Duza/Unsplash; **11** Anya Semenoff/ The Denver Post via Getty Images; **12, 13** The Granger Collection/ Alamy Stock Photo; **14** Hi Story/Alamy Stock Photo; **15** National Gallery of Art Washington. Gift of Edgar William and Bernice Chrysler Garbisch; **16** Library of Congress, Prints and Photographs Division; **18** The Granger Collection/Alamy Stock Photo; **19b, 20a** Gado Images/Alamy Stock Photo; **20b** Arthur Miller/Alamy Stock Photo; **21** U.S. National Archives and Records

Administration, Department of Commerce, Patent Office
(1925–1975); **22** Digital First Media Group/The Mercury News via
Getty Images; **25** Andrew Caballero-Reynolds/AFP via Getty
Images; **27l** CTRd/iStock; **27cl** Panchof/iStock; **27cr** Domnicky/
iStock; **27r** Viorika/iStock; **28** Luke Sharrett/Bloomberg via
Getty Images; **29** Ben Pruchnie Studio/iStock; **30** Mont592/
Shutterstock; **33** alexeys/iStock; **34** ilbusca/iStock; **35** Antiqua
Print Gallery/Alamy Stock Photo; **36** Library of Congress, Prints
and Photographs Division; **37b** Cincinnati Museum Center/Getty
Images; **38** IcemanJ/iStock; **39l** SenseiAlan/Flickr (CC by 2.0);
39r The Granger Collection/Shutterstock; **40** Luke Sharrett/
Bloomberg via Getty Images; **47** dbimages/Alamy Stock Photo;
50b William Baker/GhostWorx Images/Alamy Stock Photo;
55a John Sommers II/Bloomberg via Getty Images; **55b** Bryan
Woolston/Getty Images; **57** Reuters/John Sommers II/Alamy
Stock Photo; **59** Jennie Book/Shutterstock; **65** MoreISO/iStock;
67 David Rumsey Map Collection, David Rumsey Map Center,
Stanford Libraries; **69a** Tennessee State Library and Archives;
70 Justin Sullivan/Getty Images; **71** Ed Clark/The LIFE Picture
Collection via Getty Images; **76** Rajiv Dasan/Alamy Stock Photo;
77 CNMages/Alamy Stock Photo; **87** Yarvin World Journeys/
Alamy Stock Photo; **89** Antiqua Print Gallery/Alamy Stock
Photo; **90** apic/Getty Images; **95** Adrees Latif/Reuters/Alamy
Stock Photo; **105** Tupungato/Dreamstime; **107** ilbusca/iStock; **108**
Everett Collection/Alamy Stock Photo; **110** Dorling Kindersley/
Alamy Stock Photo; **111a & b** Patrick Fallon/Bloomberg via Getty
Images; **119** Tom Collins/iStock; **121** thepalmer/iStock; **122**
Quagga Media/Alamy Stock Photo; **126** Euskera Photography/
Alamy Stock Photo; **136** krblokhin/iStock; **139** ilbusca/iStock; **140,**
141a The Granger Collection/Alamy Stock Photo; **141** Bettman/
Getty Images; **142** Andre Chung for The Washington Post via
Getty Images; **143** Jerry Jackson/Baltimore Sun/TNS/Alamy
Live News; **151** Alex Potemkin/iStock; **153** thepalmer/iStock;
154a The Granger Collection/Alamy Stock Photo; **156** John
Frost Newspapers/Alamy Stock Photo; **167** btrenkel/iStock;
169 thepalmer/iStock; **170b** gameover/Alamy Stock Photo; **170**
Theodore Koepper/FPG/Getty Images; **171** Library of Congress,
Department of Prints and Photographs; **185** Chris LaBasco/
iStock; **187** thepalmer/iStock; **188** traveler1116/iStock; **189**
Keystone France/Gamma-Rapho/Getty Images; **190** Historical
Picture Archive/Corbis via Getty Images; **201** Gabriel Shakour/
iStock; **202** Library of Congress, Department of Prints and
Photographs; **203** David Rumsey Map Collection, David Rumsey
Map Center, Stanford Libraries.

Acknowledgements

I would like to thank and acknowledge those who made this book possible. Thank you to all the distillers and brands that despite a global pandemic took the time to speak with me and provide samples of your whiskeys. It is my honour to write about the creative work that you do. I would also like to thank Octopus Publishing Group for once again trusting me to bring this book to life and to the team who has so capably transformed my manuscript into this beautiful book. Specifically, I want to thank David T Smith and Sara L Smith for continuing to inspire and for your friendship, and Erik Owens for supporting my work and growth in the spirits industry. Most importantly, I am grateful for the support, patience and sacrifice of my wife Tia and our two boys, for giving me the time and space to write – thank you.

I would also like to acknowledge all those who have struggled and experienced loss due to the coronavirus. I hope that this simple book may bring a bit of enjoyment, and join me in raising a glass in remembrance of all those we have lost.

About the author

Eric Zandona is Director of Spirits Information at the American Distilling Institute, a spirits consultant and judge for multiple international spirits competitions. He also runs the drinks website EZdrinking.com. He lives in Vancouver, Washington.